The Eugenic Marriage

Volume IV

by

W. Grant Hague

ISBN: 978-1-63923-213-0

All Rights reserved. No part of this book maybe reproduced without written permission from the publishers, except by a reviewer who may quote brief passages in a review to be printed in a newspaper or magazine.

Printed: May 2022

Cover Art By: Amit Paul

Published and Distributed By:
Lushena Books
607 Country Club Drive, Unit E
Bensenville, IL 60106
www.lushenabooksinc.com/books

ISBN: 978-1-63923-213-0

The Eugenic Marriage

A Personal Guide to the New Science of Better Living and Better Babies

By W. GRANT HAGUE, M.D.

College of Physicians and Surgeons (Columbia University), New York; Member of County Medical Society, and of the American Medical Association

In Four Volumes

VOLUME IV

New York

THE REVIEW OF REVIEWS COMPANY

1914

Copyright, 1913, by W. Grant Hague

TABLE OF CONTENTS

LIST OF ILLUSTRATIONS

Accidents and Emergencies

CHAPTER XXXIV

COMMON DISEASES OF THE NOSE, MOUTH, AND CHEST

"Catching Cold"—Sitting on the Floor—Kicking the Bed Clothes Off—Inadequate Head Covering—Subjecting Baby to Different Temperatures Suddenly—Wearing Rubbers—Direct Infection—Acute Nasal Catarrh—Acute Coryza—Acute Rhinitis—"Cold in the Head"— "Snuffles"—Treatment of Acute Nasal Catarrh, or Rhinitis, or Coryza, or "Cold in the Head," or "Snuffles"—Chronic Nasal Catarrh—Chronic Rhinitis—Chronic Discharge from the Nose—Nervous or Persistent Cough—Adenoids as a Cause of Persistent Cough—Croup—Acute Catarrhal Laryngitis—Spasmodic Croup—False Croup—Tonsilitis—Angina—Sore Throat—Symptoms of Tonsilitis—Treatment of Tonsilitis—Bronchitis in Infants—Bronchitis in Older Children—"Don'ts" in Bronchitis—Diet in Bronchitis—Inhalations in Bronchitis— External Applications in Bronchitis—Drugs in Bronchitis—Chronic or Recurrent Bronchitis—Pneumonia—Acute Broncho-pneumonia—Symptoms of Broncho-pneumonia—How to Tell When a Child has Broncho-pneumonia—Treatment of Broncho-pneumonia—The After-treatment of Broncho-pneumonia— Adenoids—How to Tell When a Child has Adenoids—Treatment of Adenoids—Nasal Hemorrhage—"Nose-bleeds"—Treatment of Nose-bleeds—Quinsy—Hiccough—Sore Mouth— Stomatitis—Treatment of Ulcers of the Mouth—Sprue— Thrush...

CHAPTER XXXV

diseases of the stomach and gastro-intestinal canal

Inflammation of the Stomach—Acute Gastritis—Persistent Vomiting—Acute Gastric Indigestion—Iced Champagne in

Persistent Vomiting—Acute Intestinal Diseases of Children—Conditions Under Which They Exist and Suggestions as to Remedial Measures—Acute Intestinal Indigestion—Symptoms of Acute Intestinal Indigestion—Treatment of Acute Intestinal Indigestion—Children with Whom Milk Does Not Agree—Chronic or Persistent Intestinal Indigestion—Acute Ileo-colitis—Dysentery— Enteritis—Entero-colitis—Inflammatory Diarrhea—Chronic Ileo-colitis—Chronic Colitis—Summer Diarrhea—Cholera Infantum—Gastro-enteritis—Acute Gastro-enteric Infection—Gastro-enteric Intoxication—Colic Appendicitis—Jaundice in Infants—Jaundice in Older Children—Catarrhal Jaundice—Gastro-duodenitis—Intestinal Worms—Worms, Thread, Pin and Tape—Rupture...

CHAPTER XXXVI

diseases of children (continued)

Mastitis or Inflammation of the Breasts in Infancy—Mastitis in Young Girls—Let Your Ears Alone—Never Box a Child's Ears—Do Not Pick the Ears—Earache—Inflammation of the Ear—Acute Otitis—Swollen Glands—Acute Adenitis—Swollen Glands in the Groin—Boils—Hives— Nettle Rash—Prickly Heat—Ringworm in the Scalp—Eczema—Poor Blood—Simple Anemia—Chlorosis— Severe Anemia—Pernicious Anemia ...

CHAPTER XXXVII

diseases of children (continued)

Rheumatism—Malaria—Rashes of Childhood—Pimples—Acne—Blackheads—Convulsions—Fits—Spasms— Bed-wetting—Enuresis—Incontinence—Sleeplessness—Disturbed Sleep—Nightmare—Night Terrors—Headache—Thumb-sucking—Biting the Finger Nails—Colon Irrigation—How to Wash Out the Bowels—A High Enema—Enema—Methods of Reducing Fever—Ice Cap—Cold Sponging—Cold Pack—The Cold Bath—Various Baths—Mustard Baths—Hot Pack—Hot Bath—Hot Air, or Vapor Bath—Bran Bath—Tepid Bath—Cold Sponge—Shower Bath—Poultices—Hot Fomentations—How to Make and How to Apply a Mustard Paste—How to Prepare and Use the Mustard Pack—Turpentine Stupes—Oiled Silk, What it is and Why it is Used ...

Diseases of Children

CHAPTER XXXVIII

infectious or contagious diseases

Rules to be Observed in the Treatment of Contagious Diseases—What Isolation Means—The Contagious Sick Room—Conduct and Dress of the Nurse—Feeding the Patient and Nurse—How to Disinfect the Clothing and Linen—How to Disinfect the Urine and Feces—How to Disinfect the Hands—Disinfection of the Room Necessary—How to Disinfect the Mouth and Nose—How to Disinfect the Throat—Receptacle for the Sputum—Care of the Skin in Contagious Diseases—Convalescence After a Contagious Disease—Disinfecting the Sick Chamber—The After Treatment of a Disinfected Room—How to Disinfect the Bed Clothing and Clothes—Mumps—Epidemic Parotitis—Chicken Pox—Varicella—La Grippe—Influenza—Diphtheria—Whooping Cough—Pertussis—Measles—Koplik's Spots—Department of Health Rules in Measles—Scarlet Fever—Scarlatina—Typhoid Fever—Various Solutions—Boracic Acid Solution—Normal Salt Solution—Carron Oil—Thiersch's Solution—Solution of Bichloride of Mercury—How to Make Various Solutions ....

Accidents and Emergencies

CHAPTER XXXIX

accidents and emergencies

Accidents and Emergencies—Contents of the Family Medicine Chest—Foreign Bodies in the Eye—Foreign Bodies in the Ear—Foreign Bodies in the Nose—Foreign Bodies in the Throat—A Bruise or Contusion—Wounds—Arrest of Hemorrhage—Removal of Foreign Bodies from a Wound—Cleansing a Wound—Closing and Dressing Wounds—The Condition of Shock—Dog Bites— Sprains— Dislocations—Wounds of the Scalp— Run-around—Felon— Whitlow—

Burns and Scalds ...

Miscellaneous

CHAPTER XL

miscellaneous

The Dangerous House Fly—Diseases Transmitted by Flies—Homes Should be Carefully Screened and Protected—The Breeding Places of Flies—Special Care Should be Given to Stables, Privy Vaults, Garbage, Vacant Lots, Foodstuffs, Water Fronts, Drains—Precautions to be Observed—How to Kill Flies—Moths—What Physicians are Doing—Radium—X-Ray Treatment and X-Ray Diagnosis—Aseptic Surgery—New Anesthetics—Vaccine in Typhoid Fever—"606"—Transplanting the Organs of Dead Men into the Living—Bacteria that Make Soil Barren or Productive—Antimeningitis Serum—A Serum for Malaria in Sight ...

CHAPTER XXXIV

COMMON DISEASES OF THE NOSE, MOUTH, AND CHEST

"Catching Cold"—Sitting on the Floor— Kicking the Bed Clothes Off—Inadequate Head Covering—Subjecting Baby to Different Temperatures Suddenly—Wearing Rubbers—Direct Infection—Acute Nasal Catarrh—Acute Coryza—Acute Rhinitis—"Cold in the Head"—"Snuffles"— Treatment of Acute Nasal Catarrh, or Rhinitis, or Coryza, or "Cold in the Head," or "Snuffles"—Chronic Nasal Catarrh—Chronic Rhinitis—Chronic Discharge from the Nose—Nervous or Persistent Cough — Adenoids as a Cause of Persistent Cough—Croup—Acute Catarrhal Laryngitis—Spasmodic Croup—False Croup—Tonsilitis—Angina—Sore Throat—Symptoms of Tonsilitis—Treatment of Tonsilitis—Bronchitis in Infants— Bronchitis in Older Children—"Don'ts" in Bronchitis—Diet in Bronchitis—Inhalations in Bronchitis—External Applications in Bronchitis—Drugs in Bronchitis—Chronic or Recurrent Bronchitis—

Pneumonia—Acute Broncho-pneumonia—Symptoms of Broncho-pneumonia—How to Tell When a Child has Broncho-pneumonia—Treatment of Broncho-pneumonia—The After-treatment of Broncho-pneumonia—Adenoids—How to Tell When a Child has Adenoids—Treatment of Adenoids—Nasal Hemorrhage—"Nose-bleeds"—Treatment of Nose-bleeds—Quinsy—Hiccough—Sore Mouth— Stomatitis—Treatment of Ulcers of the Mouth—Sprue—Thrush.

"CATCHING COLDS"

Mothers frequently wonder where their children get colds. Briefly we will point out some of the sources from which these apparently inexplicable colds may come.

A. Sitting on the Floor.—Children should not be allowed to sit or crawl upon the floor at any season of the year, but especially during the winter months. There is always a draught of cold air near the floor. It is a bad habit to begin allowing a child to play with its toys on the floor. Use the bed or a sofa or a platform raised a foot from the floor.

[498] **B. Kicking the Bed Clothes Off During the Night.**—The bed clothes should be securely pinned to the mattress by large safety pins. When it is established as a habit a child who kicks off the bed clothes should wear a combination night suit with "feet," made of flannel during the winter and of cotton during the summer.

C. Inadequate Head Covering.—Professor Kerley states that this is one of the "most frequent causes of disease of the respiratory tract in the young." He calls attention to the fact that "mothers carefully clothe the baby with ample coats, blankets, leggings, etc., before they take him out for the daily walk. They dress him in a warm room taking plenty of time to put on the extra clothes, during which time the baby frets and perspires. When all is ready they place upon the hot, almost bald head of the baby a light artistically decorated airy creation which is sold in the shops as children's caps. The child is then taken out of doors and because of the inadequate covering of the hot perspiring head, catches cold and the mother never knows how it came." Every baby and child should wear under such caps a skull cap of thin flannel, especially in cold weather. In summer or windy day a light silk handkerchief folded under the cap is a very excellent protection.

D. Subjecting a Baby to Different Temperatures Suddenly, is liable to be followed by a cold—for example, taking the child from a warm room to a cold room, or through a cold hall, holding the child at an open window for a few moments.

E. The Practice of Wearing Rubbers Needs Some Consideration.—They should never be worn indoors for even five minutes. They should not therefore be kept on in school, nor should they be worn by women in stores when they go shopping. When it is actually raining, or snowing, or when there is slush or wet mud they are needful; but they should not be worn simply because the weather is threatening or damp. Children should not put them on to play—worn for any length of time when active they are harmful. If worn to and from school they should be taken off at once when in school or at home. Wearing rubbers prevents free evaporation of the natural [499] secretion of the skin, keeps the feet moist and invites colds and catarrh. In damp weather, or when children play during winter months, they should be shod with stout shoes with cork insoles.

The same argument applies to storm coats of rubber, water-proof material. They should not be worn as overcoats all day, but only when going to and from school or business when it is actually storming.

Underclothing or hosiery should not be heavy enough to cause moisture of the skin. Health demands a dry skin at all times. The necessary degree of body heat should be attained by the quality of the outer clothing, not by the quantity of the underclothing. Many men and women wear heavy underclothing which causes moisture when indoors, with the result that they get surface chills when they go outside if the weather is cold and as a result catch cold. The underclothing should be just heavy enough to be comfortable indoors and the extra warmth necessary when outside should be supplied by a good overcoat or furs.

F. Direct Infection.—A baby may catch cold if kissed or "hugged" by an adult who has a cold.

Catching cold while bathing is possible, but scarcely probable, if ordinary precautions are taken. It is very bad practice to permit children to use one another's handkerchiefs or the handkerchief of an adult. Certain children are predisposed to attacks of "cold in the head" or acute coryza or nasal catarrh (these being the medical names for this condition). Sometimes this is an inherited characteristic. There is no doubt, however, that most of these children acquire the habit by bad sanitary and hygienic surroundings. These children do not as a rule get enough fresh air. They are kept indoors most of the time in stuffy, overheated, badly ventilated rooms, unless the weather is absolutely perfect. The windows in their bedrooms are always kept closed, because they are "liable to catch cold." They are overdressed and perspire easily and as a result "catch cold." These conditions all tend to create an unhealthy condition of the nasal mucous membrane and of the throat, and this is rendered worse if the child lives in a damp, changeable climate, such as [500] that of New York City. In these susceptible children the exciting cause of an attack may be trivial; exposure, cold or wet feet, inadequate head covering (as already pointed out), a draught of cold air even may excite sneezing and a nasal discharge; hence we have:

Acute Nasal Catarrh (Acute Coryza, Acute Rhinitis, "Cold in the Head", "Snuffles").—Acute nasal catarrh may accompany measles, diphtheria, influenza, and whooping cough.

Symptoms.—The onset is sudden with sneezing, and difficulty in breathing through the nose. In a few hours, or it may be not for a day or two, a mucous, watery, nasal discharge appears. There are redness and slight swelling of the nose and upper lip, caused by the discharge. There is no fever as a general rule except in very young infants, in whom the fever may be very high. The discharge interferes with the nursing and the child suffers from lack of nourishment. The inflammation may extend to the eyes and ears, causing painful complications, or to the throat and bronchi, causing hoarseness and cough. Less frequently we have disturbances of the digestive tract with vomiting, or diarrhea.

The mild form of the disease lasts for two or three days, the severe form from one to two weeks.

Repeated attacks are said to contribute to the production of adenoid growths.

An acute attack of this disease is seldom a serious affliction in older children; it may be, however, very serious and even dangerous in very young infants. The tendency of the disease to extend downward, causing bronchitis or pneumonia, explains in part the possible danger to a baby. Another reason is because it may seriously interfere with suckling and with breathing in these little patients. It may even cause sudden attacks of strangulation.

An infant, therefore, suffering with an acute attack of rhinitis requires constant attention. It may be necessary to feed it with a spoon, and if necessary mother's milk should be so fed. Plenty of fresh air should be provided. It may be essential to keep the mouth open in order that it may get enough fresh air. Every effort should be made to keep the nostrils open. The secretions must be removed [501] from time to time. Causing the child to sneeze by tickling the nose with a camel's hair brush will clear the nose for the time being. The physician may be compelled to use a solution of cocaine for this purpose.

Treatment of Acute Rhinitis ("Taking Cold", Nasal Catarrh, Acute Coryza, "Snuffles").—A child suffering with an acute attack of "cold in the head" should be kept indoors in a room with a constant, uniform temperature; the particular reason for this is, that, if a child is exposed to cold at any time during an attack of "cold in the head," it may cause the disease to invade the chest,—a tendency which it has at all times. The bowels must be kept open; if they do not move every day of their own accord they must be made to move by means of an enema of sweet oil or of soap-suds. The amount of food should be reduced to suit the circumstances and the condition of the patient.

We treat the local condition in the nose with a menthol mixture. The following is a very good one: Menthol, 30 grains; Camphor, 30 grains; White Vaseline, 1 ounce. Put some of this on the end of the finger and push it gently into each nostril. When the nostrils become blocked and the child cannot breathe through the nose, tickle the nose with a feather until it sneezes; this will clear the passage. Immediately after the sneeze place the menthol mixture in each nostril. When the child is about to sneeze place a handkerchief before the nose, as this discharge is full of germs and will infect others when dry. Internal remedies should not be used unless the child is distinctly sick and is running a fever, in which case a physician should look the child over and prescribe whatever is called for.

The upper lip and the nostrils of the child should be protected, because the discharge very quickly irritates the parts and renders them raw and painful. Vaseline or cold cream is very suitable for this purpose.

Mothers should not wash out the nose of a child with any solution advised for this purpose where force is used, as, for example, with a syringe. Any forceful irrigation of the nose is dangerous, because it would carry the infection into the deeper parts and set up a more serious condition. [502]

If the above treatment is carefully carried out and the child unexposed to a fresh cold, two or three days will be sufficient to cure the disease.

It is not, however, the treatment of an acute attack of "cold in the head" that is important; it is intelligently to follow out a plan which will prevent these attacks from repeating themselves that is of consequence. The tendency to take cold is a real condition in childhood and a very common one. When mothers appreciate that it is possible to prevent this condition and to cure it when it is seemingly an established habit, more interest will undoubtedly be taken in the subject. Too frequently it is looked upon as an unfortunate affliction, but it is never regarded as a condition that is caused by neglect and ignorance.

It is an exceedingly common occurence to find a mother worrying over her child's cold, dosing it with cod liver oil or some other unnecessary tonic, rubbing it with camphorated oil or plastering it over with certain useless patent plasters, dressing it with extra pieces of flannel on its chest and extra clothes pinned snugly around it, then shutting it up in a warm, stuffy, unsanitary, ill-smelling room, in order to keep it from "catching a fresh cold." Can you imagine anything else she could do to defeat her purpose?

No quantity of cod liver oil, no medicine, no coddling, will remove the tendency to "catch cold." The child's life must be lived amidst sanitary surroundings and hygienic conditions first; then other expedients may be utilized if necessary. These children must be kept out of doors most of the time, unless during the severest wet weather. They should sleep in a room the windows of which are open at the top and bottom every night in the year. They should not, however, be in a draught. The rooms in which they live should be of a uniform temperature, never too hot and never too cold, between 68° and 70° F. These delicate catarrhal children should be accustomed to light clothing on their beds. Chest protectors, mufflers, cotton pads, and heavy wraps of any description should be absolutely prohibited. It is advisable to use flannel underwear winter and summer, light in summer and a medium weight in winter. [503] During the summer months the mother should begin cold sponging of the face, throat, chest, and spine every morning and carry it into the winter. The entire process need take only a moment or two. Always dry thoroughly with a fairly rough towel. If the cold sponging is begun in the warm summer time the child will become so accustomed to it that no objection will be made when the cold weather comes.

If the child continues to be "catarrhal," despite a course of this treatment, it would be well to investigate whether any adenoids or adenoid tissue exist in the naso-pharynx. If adenoids are found no treatment will be successful until they are removed.

It is a wise plan to place a flannel cap on an infant who has an acute attack of "cold in the head" (snuffles). This will prevent catching a fresh cold and it will aid in the speedy cure of the attack from which it is suffering when it is put on.

CHRONIC NASAL CATARRH—CHRONIC RHINITIS CHRONIC DISCHARGE FROM THE NOSE

Some children have a nasal discharge during all of their childhood. It is usually worse during the winter months. It may be a thin, watery discharge or a thick, nasty, yellow discharge.

It is a condition that is very frequently neglected even by the family physician. This is unfortunate because it may lead to serious disease, permanent damage sometimes being done to the hearing, the speech, the smell, and to the lungs of the child.

It may be caused by adenoids; disease of the bones or tissues in the nose; foreign bodies in the nose; or it may occur in children whose nutrition is bad. It may result from frequent acute attacks of "cold in the head." It also occurs in other less important conditions. The foreign bodies which usually cause a chronic nasal discharge are,—buttons, peas, beans, beads, paper balls, flies and bugs, cherry-stones, small pieces of coal, or stone, cork or other material. A child gets hold of a shoe-button for example and pushes it into its nostrils. In the effort [504] to get it out the child pushes it further in. It may or may not cause pain at the time, and it may be overlooked, but shortly the mother will notice a discharge from one nostril. This discharge becomes thick and foul and when an investigation is made the button is found embedded firmly in the nose. It is sometimes quite difficult to get the button out and this should always be done by a physician.

Treatment.—Remove the cause first then treat the catarrh. If it is a product of a constitutional disease that causes general poor health, such as tuberculosis, syphilis, or scrofula, the child will need "building up" and a decided change of climate. Foreign bodies must be removed, adenoids taken out, large tonsils excised, and malformations of the nasal bones operated upon. The catarrh will in many cases be cured by removing its cause; if, however, it should persist it must be treated for some time with appropriate solutions. These solutions and the directions as to the method of giving them must be given by a physician, because there is great danger of carrying the disease to deeper structures if given wrongly.

SUMMARY:—

1st.—A chronic discharge from the nose is a sign that something is wrong and should be carefully and thoroughly investigated.

2nd.—The cause can usually be found out and the proper treatment will cure it.

3rd.—If the condition is neglected it may ruin the health of the child for the whole period of its life.

NERVOUS OR PERSISTENT COUGH

Cough in an infant or growing child is usually the result of a cold and the structure affected is some part of the nose, throat or bronchi. It is a comparatively simple matter to discover just where the trouble is and to prescribe the appropriate remedy and effect a cure.

There is another type of cough, however, that is of [505] quite a different character. This cough will begin as an ordinary cough and it will only be discovered that it is not an ordinary cough because nothing will apparently cure it. We mean that the child is given cough remedies that usually cure a cold, is kept in the house and carefully watched for a sufficiently long period to justify a cure, and yet, despite this care and attention, the cough remains the same. The child is not sick, the appetite is good, there is no fever, it plays and seems to enjoy good health, yet for weeks and frequently for months the annoying cough hangs on. It is as a rule worse at night. It begins soon after the child falls asleep and spoils the entire night's rest or a great part of it. It may be a dry, hard, hacking cough, or a croupy, harsh bark. It may come in spells with a considerable interval between them, during which time the child falls asleep, or it may be almost constant, not quite severe enough to rouse the child, but bad enough to spoil the child's rest and the rest of the mother. If this condition lasts for a long time, as it occasionally does, the health of the little patient is apt to suffer from loss of sleep.

Treatment.—These children should be taken to a good physician and thoroughly examined. Special care should be devoted to investigating the condition of the nose, throat, ear, stomach, heart, and lungs.

A very large majority of these coughs are caused by adenoid growths in the back part of the nose. The child may not look like an adenoid child, nor may it breathe through its mouth when asleep, and it may have had its adenoids removed, yet in spite of these contra-indications it may have enough loose adenoid tissue in its nose to cause this kind of persistent cough. This has been proved many times.

It is not only useless but positively harmful to give these children cough remedies. The cause of the cough must be found and treated. The cough may be indirectly caused by anemia (poor blood) or heart or stomach trouble, or it may have a number of other causes. Whatever it is it must be found by a careful physical examination or a number of careful physical examinations, because these cases are as a rule obscure and difficult [506] to diagnose, and even the most expert examiner cannot always tell where the trouble is without seeing the child a number of times. The parents must therefore have patience and confidence in the physician and must aid him all they can by watching and reporting all the symptoms, etc., to him. (See article on Adenoids).

SUMMARY:—

Coughs that resist careful treatment are not "ordinary coughs."

Coughs of this type require special medical care.

The usual cough medicines are not only useless in these coughs, but dangerous. Don't give them.

ACUTE CATARRHAL LARYNGITIS: SPASMODIC CROUP: FALSE CROUP

Croup is one of the common diseases of childhood. It usually follows a catarrhal "cold in the head" with a cough. Croup is most frequently associated with large tonsils and adenoids. It may come on gradually or it may occur suddenly. There is always fever with croup. One of the first symptoms is a hard, dry, croupy, barking cough, which gets worse toward night. If it occurs suddenly, the child will wake about midnight with the characteristic croupy cough. The disease may go no further than this and under the proper treatment is well in a few days. In other cases, however, there develops marked interference with breathing. Every inspiration is accompanied by a loud hissing or "crowing" sound. This feature of the disease is one that frightens the parents, though it seldom means anything serious. The child sits up in bed, frightened, and struggles for breath. It may clutch its throat with its hands as if something was tied round its neck. The lips may become slightly blue and the perspiration appears upon the child's brow. After some time,—it may be two or three hours,—the attack wears away and the child goes to sleep. Next morning it wakes up apparently well except for the croupy cough. The attack may repeat itself the next night and mildly on the third night. [507]

Treatment.—The object of treatment during an acute attack, when the child is struggling for breath, is to relax quickly the spasm of the larynx which interferes with the breathing. The simplest way is to give the child a teaspoonful of the fresh syrup of ipecac. If the child does not vomit in fifteen minutes, give another teaspoonful and keep on giving it every fifteen minutes till the child vomits. One or two doses is usually enough, but it must be given till the child vomits.

If the attack comes suddenly during the night and there is no syrup of ipecac in the house, the physician should be sent for at once and informed that the child probably has croup, so he may know what to take with him. While waiting for the physician the mother should apply over the front of the neck (in the region of Adam's apple), hot applications. These are best made of flannel wrung out of quite hot water every two or three minutes: also a hot mustard foot bath. When the physician takes charge of the case he will also direct the treatment for the following day in order that the attack of the next night may be a very mild one, if it should came at all.

Children who have a tendency to frequent attacks of croup should receive the same attention as the children do who are subject to attacks of tonsilitis and acute catarrhal rhinitis.

SUMMARY:—

1st. Spasmodic Croup always requires prompt and efficient treatment.

2nd. It is called "false" croup, because "true" croup is always diphtheritic and is a very serious disease.

3rd. For that reason a physician should always be called because if it is "true" croup antitoxin must be given at once.

4th. Don't worry unnecessarily because, though "spasmodic croup" can make the child look exceedingly sick for a very short time, an uncomplicated case in a healthy child is seldom if ever dangerous. [508]

TONSILITIS: ANGINA: "SORE THROAT"

This is one of the frequent diseases of childhood. We rarely see it in infants. It is caused by inhaling air which contains poisonous germs. These germs quickly develop when conditions are favorable. They lodge in the pores or follicles of the tonsils and set up an active inflammation. The tonsils swell up and the follicles exude a thick fluid which looks like curdled cream. This fluid sticks in the mouths of the follicles forming spots. If enough of this fluid is coming out, these spots join together forming patches, and the patches may join together forming membrane. This is why it is sometimes so difficult to tell whether the case is one of tonsilitis or diphtheria.

Conditions are favorable to the development of tonsilitis if the child is not in good health when he happens to inhale the infection, when the feet are wet or cold, or when the child is allowed out during inclement weather and it becomes chilled or numbed from cold, when the child has a cold in the head and a running nose, or when its stomach is out of order. Any condition in which the child should be carefully watched and tended to, rather than allowed further liberties, or risks, conduces to sore throat of some kind.

Some children have the disease a number of times; they seem to be predisposed toward a sore throat. These are children who have large tonsils or who are rheumatic. The tonsils should be removed in the one case, and the tendency to rheumatism should be the main treatment in the other case.

These children should be encouraged to cleanse the throat and nose morning and night with a warm salt solution (half a teaspoonful of ordinary table salt to three-quarters of a cup of warm water). This will help greatly to prevent these chronic sore throats.

Symptoms of Tonsilitis.—The disease begins suddenly. The child may have a chill or be seized with sudden vomiting or diarrhea. A very young infant may have a convulsion. The usual way is for the child to develop a fever quickly, to complain of being sick and tired. Muscular pains all over the body and a severe headache [509] are constant symptoms. The fever is usually high from the beginning. The child will tell you its throat is sore, but there is as a rule very little pain in the throat. The little spots or patches can be seen on one or both tonsils. The general symptoms are more pronounced than the local throat symptoms. The amount of physical depression that is caused by a tonsilitis is out of all proportion to the seriousness of the disease.

Tonsilitis lasts three days usually. The throat symptoms may take a day or two longer to clear up, and the patients feel more or less weak for some time after all the symptoms have disappeared.

Tonsilitis is medically regarded as one of the mild diseases of childhood. It is, however, of very great importance because of its likeness to diphtheria, and inasmuch as a positive diagnosis must be promptly made, in the interest of the patient, it is given close attention and treated with considerable respect by the medical profession. The chief differences between the two diseases are as follows:

Tonsilitis begins abruptly with pronounced prostration and a high fever the first day. The patient feels distinctly sick all over. The second day the patient feels somewhat better, the fever is lower and the prostration and pain are not so marked. The third day he feels better still, and but for a little weakness would feel well. Diphtheria begins slowly and insidiously, with very little prostration and a very low fever the first day. The patient scarcely feels sick. The second day more prostration is present, the fever climbs upward a little more, and the patient begins to feel sick. On the third day the prostration is much more profound, the fever is higher, and all the evidences of a serious sickness are present. Two very different pictures: The one begins bad and ends easy, the other begins easy and may end bad.

The important fact, however, so far as the similarity of the two diseases is concerned, is, that we must make the diagnosis positive on the first or second day, because if we are dealing with a case of diphtheria we must give antitoxin at once. This is essential, because the efficacy of antitoxin is greatest when given early in the [510] disease. By "early" we mean the first or second day of the disease. When antitoxin is given late (the third or fourth day of the disease) it is much less efficacious and must be given in relatively larger doses. The need, therefore, of a quick, positive diagnosis is a real one.

Another important element involved in a speedy diagnosis is, that we must not take any chances of infecting other children. So important are these conditions that it is the proper treatment to give antitoxin at once in every case of tonsilitis that in the slightest way resembles diphtheria. An examination of the throat contents,—a culture of which is taken during the first visit of the physician,—will, of course, reveal the true condition and dictate the future use of the antitoxin. Antitoxin is absolutely harmless when given to a patient who has no diphtheria. Every case of tonsilitis should be quarantined when there are other children in the house.

The local condition of the throat helps in the diagnosis: In tonsilitis (as the name implies) the disease is limited to the tonsils and on the tonsils (one or both) do we find the spots or patches. In diphtheria, on the other hand, the membrane is not limited to the tonsils, but may cover every part of the throat and extend into the nose and mouth. In tonsilitis it is spots or patches we see in the throat. In diphtheria it is membrane we see always. The difficulty here again is that if we wait till the diphtheritic membrane covers the whole throat, antitoxin will not be of much use.

In diphtheria we have a characteristic odor, in tonsilitis we have no characteristic odor.

The practical lesson to be learned from this uncertainty is, immediately to get a physician as soon as you find spots in the throat of your sick child, unless you are absolutely sure that the condition is not diphtheria and you are willing to take that chance.

Treatment of an Acute Attack of Tonsilitis.—Put the child in bed at once and keep him on a light diet during the fever. Give him all the cool boiled water he wants to drink. If the fever is very high it can be controlled by sponging the body with cool water. If the patient is an infant the food should be reduced to one-half [511] strength. Tonsilitis is a disease that runs a certain course and gets better, or the patient develops some other more serious conditions as a result of neglect or carelessness. We therefore try to make the patient comfortable and let the disease take care of itself.

The throat can be gargled or sprayed with any mild antiseptic liquid, or it can be painted with tincture of iodine or 10 per cent. solution of silver nitrate. As a rule the gargles do not aid in the cure of the disease, though they contribute to the comfort of the patient.

A cold compress made of half a dozen thicknesses of cloth, such as a table napkin, and put under the jaw (not round the neck), and covered with oiled silk and held in place with a bandage that meets and is tied on the top of the head, is of distinct usefulness.

When it is known that the child is rheumatic, the heart must be carefully watched during the fever and anti-rheumatic remedies depended upon to effect a cure.

SUMMARY:—

Tonsilitis, because of its likeness to diphtheria, must be promptly and carefully diagnosed.

A physician only is capable of making a diagnosis.

Any sore throat in a child with spots or membrane is deserving of serious and immediate attention.

A mistake may mean death. Don't take a chance.

BRONCHITIS

Bronchitis is one of the commonest diseases of childhood. It is the cause of many deaths. Exposure during inclement weather is as a rule the cause of it. It occurs in all classes and conditions of children. Poorly nourished and badly clothed children are more liable to get it than are others. It is more dangerous in young children and infants than in older children. A young child or an infant will get bronchitis quicker than those older and stronger under the same conditions.

Bronchitis is often present while children are suffering from other diseases, measles, influenza, scarlet fever, typhoid fever, pneumonia, diphtheria, whooping-cough, for example. It may accompany any disease of childhood, however.[512]

Symptoms.—In infants bronchitis usually follows a "cold in the head," with running nose and a cough. The child is indisposed and peevish because of the cold. In a few days the cough becomes worse, fever develops, the breathing is quicker, and the baby looks and acts sick. The cough may be constant and severe; sometimes the cough does not seem to bother the baby, although this is exceptional. The breathing is quite rapid and is accompanied with a moist, rattling sound in the chest. The baby is restless and if the cough is severe it becomes exhausted. Vomiting or diarrhea may be present.

Bronchitis in Older Children.—Bronchitis in older children comes on abruptly, with fever and cough. The child may complain of headache and pains in the chest or other parts of the body. It may begin with a chill or chilly feelings. These children "raise" with the cough. The expectoration may be quite profuse; at first it is a white, frothy mucus, then yellow, and later a yellowish green; it may be slightly tinged with blood.

There is a mild form of bronchitis in these older children where the serious symptoms are absent. The children are not sick enough to go to bed, but they appear to have a "heavy cold" with, at first, a tight, hard cough, which is usually worse at night. Later the cough turns loose and the same expectoration occurs as in the severe type. It is these cases of mild bronchitis which do not receive the proper care and treatment that develop into the so-called "winter cough," which lasts for months.

Treatment.—(See page 497 under heading, "Catching Colds.") Children who acquire bronchitis easily and frequently, should be built up. Cod liver oil should be given all winter. The sleeping apartment of these children should not be too cold, but it should be well aired through the day and well ventilated throughout the night. Flannel night clothes should be worn and the feet should be kept warm always. Mild attacks of "cold in the head" should be treated vigorously and not neglected.

The following "Don'ts" may be profitably studied when your child or baby has bronchitis:—

[513]

Don't keep the windows tightly closed; fresh air and good ventilation are absolutely necessary to the patient.
Don't use a cotton jacket or oil silk.
Don't wrap the child up in blankets and shawls.
Don't carry the child around; keep it in bed.
Don't dose the child with syrupy cough mixtures.
Don't overheat the room.
Don't let friends bother or annoy the baby.
Don't reduce the diet unnecessarily.

The child should be put to bed. The temperature of the room should be 70 degrees F. all the time. The windows should be opened top and bottom according to the weather, and the room should be well aired every day, the patient being taken to another room while it is being done. The child should have its usual night clothes on, nothing more. If the child is not very sick and insists on sitting up, a bath robe can be worn but it should be always removed when it sleeps. It is advisable to change the position of the baby from time to time. Have it rest on one side, then on the other, as well as on the back. Give a dose of castor oil at the beginning of the sickness and keep the bowels open during the disease.

Diet.—The diet will depend upon the severity of the disease. If the fever is high and the cough persistent, the strength of the food of nursing infants should be reduced. We can reduce the strength of the food by giving the child a drink of cool boiled water before each feeding and shortening the length of each feeding. Older children may be given toast, milk with lime water, cocoa with milk, broths, gruels, custards, cereals and fruit juices.

Inhalations.—The value of inhalations in bronchitis is very great. The ordinary croup kettle, which can be bought in any good drug store, is the best method of giving them. Full directions come with each kettle as to the best way to use it. The best drug to use in the kettle is creosote (beechwood). Ten drops are added to one quart of boiling water and the steaming continued for thirty minutes. The interval between steaming is two hours and a half in bad cases day and night. In mild cases the night treatments can be dispensed with. Sheets rigged up over the top and sides of the crib, in [514] the form of a tent, is the most desirable way to give the inhalations.

External Applications.—Counter-irritation by means of mustard pastes are the best applications. They should be put back and front—one on back and one on the chest, overlapping at the sides beneath the arms. They should cover the entire body from the waist line to the neck. These pastes are made as follows:— Mix the mustard (English) and the flour in the following proportions, using a quantity according to the size of child and area to be covered; one tablespoonful mustard to three tablespoonfuls of flour. Mix with lukewarm water until a paste is formed, not too thick and not too thin. Spread on a cloth (put plenty on) and cover with one layer of cheesecloth and place the cheesecloth side next the skin. In order to guard against burning the skin it is advisable to rub the skin with vaseline, before and after putting on the paste. The paste should be left on until the skin is uniformly red. It may be applied from two to four times in the twenty-four hours according to the severity of the case. Mustard pastes are most effective during the first two or three days of the disease.

Drugs.—Drugs are of very little value in the treatment of bronchitis. In the first stage of the disease, when the cough is hard and dry, small doses of castor oil and syrup of ipecac may be given to good advantage. The following dosage should be followed closely: 1st year, 2 drops castor oil, 2 drops syrup of ipecac, every two hours; 3rd year, 3 drops castor oil, 3 drops syrup of ipecac, every two hours; over 3 years, 4 drops castor oil, 4 drops syrup of ipecac, every two hours.

The benefits from this treatment will be obtained in the first two or three days, when it should be discontinued. The cough under this treatment and the use of the mustard paste and inhalations of creosote will be soft and loose in two or three days and the fever will be distinctly on the mend. The disease lasts from five to ten days. It may, however, last much longer according to the condition of the child, etc.

There are other drugs that can be given, with good effect, but when other remedies are indicated a physician [515] should be called to prescribe them according to indications.

SUMMARY:—

Bronchitis is one of the commonest diseases of childhood.

It is the cause of many deaths.

A large number of children have a tendency to bronchitis.

These children need careful attention and "building up."

Do not neglect a "little" cold. It means trouble.

Chronic or Recurrent Bronchitis.—Bronchitis becomes chronic when the treatment of an acute attack fails to cure the condition. The failure usually is dependent upon the condition of the child. It may be suffering with some disease resulting from poor nourishment or poor sanitary and hygienic surroundings or both. The bronchitis, in other words, is dependent upon some other condition, and will not get wholly better until the cause is cured. These children should lead an active outdoor life when the weather is favorable. Their sleeping-room should be well aired and ventilated. Red meats are allowed twice a week only. Sugar is cut down to the lowest limit. Skimmed milk only should be taken—the cream being too rich for them. They can eat freely of fruits in season, green vegetables and cereals. The bowels must move freely every day. Patients must be given a lukewarm bath, followed by a brief spray of cold water, daily. The cold spray should not be too cold; about 60 degrees F. is the suitable temperature of the water.

An absolute change of climate, to a warmer inland atmosphere, is imperative before some of these patients will begin to improve.

SUMMARY:—

A child with chronic bronchitis, or with frequent attacks of bronchitis (or chronic colds), is usually suffering from some other diseased condition.

The bronchitis, or the cold, will not get better until [516] you find out what that "other diseased condition" is.

It takes a physician to find that out.

Having found the cause, cure it, and the bronchitis will disappear and the general health of the child will immediately improve.

PNEUMONIA

Pneumonia is a very common disease in childhood. It is the most frequent complication of the various acute infectious diseases. Pneumonia is an exceedingly important factor in the mortality of infancy.

There are two kinds of pneumonia:—

1. Broncho-pneumonia.
2. Lobar-pneumonia.

Acute Broncho-Pneumonia.—Up to the fourth year this is the form of pneumonia always present. It is the form that always complicates other diseases all through childhood.

It is most apt to occur during the spring and winter months.

It affects all classes, but especially those whose hygienic surroundings are poor. Catching cold is the exciting cause in a large percentage of primary pneumonias.

Symptoms.—Broncho-pneumonia has no regular course. It may or it may not follow a cold or an attack of bronchitis. As a rule it begins suddenly with a high fever, frequently accompanied by vomiting, rapid respiration, cough, and prostration.

The child does not maintain a high fever continuously; it varies considerably throughout each twenty-four hours. It lasts from one to three weeks, and subsides gradually.

The respirations vary between 60 and 80 per minute, though they may be much more frequent than this. The child breathes with apparent difficulty, the soft parts of the cheeks and nose rising and falling as it breathes.

The prostration becomes, as the disease progresses, more and more marked, until the child looks profoundly sick.

Cough is a constant and incessant symptom. It disturbs rest and sleep and may cause frequent vomiting. [517] There is no expectoration. A strong cough is a good symptom; if it stops it is a bad symptom.

Pain is seldom present.

Blueness of the skin is a bad sign and indicates failure of respiration and suggests constant and careful watching.

Delirium may be present during the disease. It is not necessarily a bad sign. Accompanying stomach troubles are frequent if the patient is very young, and are very important. The bowels may be loose; they may be green in color and contain much mucus. Large quantities of gas may accumulate in the intestines and may cause much distress and convulsions. Death may occur at any time or the process may be arrested and recovery take place at any stage of the disease. Broncho-pneumonia is not necessarily a fatal disease in a fairly healthy child. It is, however, always a serious disease.

Various complications may occur in the course of the disease. The most frequent are: pleurisy, emphysema, abscess of the lung, meningitis, heart disease, stomach troubles, thrush, intestinal disease.

How to Tell When a Child Has Broncho-Pneumonia.—If a child develops a high fever, breathes rapidly, coughs, and is content to lie in bed because of the degree of prostration, broncho-pneumonia is almost certain to be the disease present. If in addition to these symptoms there is any blueness of the fingers or around the mouth it is more strongly suggestive of pneumonia.

If the child has been suffering with bronchitis it is sometimes difficult to tell just when the pneumonia begins. The child will appear more profoundly sick, the fever will go higher, and the respiration will be more frequent when pneumonia sets in on top of bronchitis.

Treatment.—The nursing of a little patient with pneumonia is the most important part. He must get plenty of fresh air; consequently he should be kept in a well-ventilated room. It is an excellent plan to change the patient twice daily from the sick room into another which has previously been thoroughly aired. While he is in this room the sick room should be as thoroughly aired as is possible. Keep this plan up all through the disease; change the position of the patient in bed every two hours. [518] He should never be allowed to lie on his back for hours at a time. In this way the different parts of the lungs get a chance to air themselves,—the air cells expand and the oxygen in the air and the fresh blood tend to heal the parts more quickly.

It would be distinctly wrong to go into the detailed symptomatic treatment of broncho-pneumonia in a book of this character. Inasmuch as this is one of the most serious diseases of infancy, no mother should attempt to treat it alone. A physician is absolutely necessary and the most the mother can hope to do is to follow out his directions to the letter.

He may direct the use of mustard pastes but it is essential to know where to apply them. If he should request the use of the cotton jacket, the height and character of the fever must regulate its use. Stimulants are always necessary, whisky and strychnine being given in every case, but if given at the wrong time they may do more harm than good. Cough mixtures may be necessary, but frequently they are contra-indicated. Drugs and cold sponging may be used to reduce the fever, but they are dangerous if used when conditions do not justify their use.

Complications must be diagnosed when they occur, and the correct methods of treatment promptly instituted. A competent physician alone can assume the responsibility of these various phases of the disease.

Every mother should appreciate, however, that pneumonia is frequently the result of carelessness. It is a well-known fact that pneumonia is an infrequent disease among children of the well-to-do, because the hygienic surroundings of these children are better and because they receive competent attention if suffering with colds and bronchitis. Bronchitis is quite common in all classes of children, but in the lower walks of life it is the custom to allow children to run around while they give every sign of having a heavy cold, and a beginning bronchitis. These children should receive treatment and should be kept indoors and in bed if they have even a slight fever, as pneumonia is frequently the inevitable outcome. They should be carefully fed, and all signs of stomach or intestinal troubles attended to at once. [518f]

By permission of Henry H. Goddard A Grim Result Isaac is 16, although mentally 10. He is a high-grade moron.

This is one of those all too frequent instances[A] "of a feeble-minded woman with a husband who is alcoholic and the offspring either feeble-minded or miscarriages."

"Isaac is exceedingly dangerous. He is a potential criminal or bad man, or under the best conditions would at least marry and probably become the father of defectives like himself."

This and the succeeding pictures in this volume contrast vividly with the frontispiece. Terrible are the results when we disregard the inevitable laws of nature, and so mate ourselves that our children will be parasites on society.

[A]"Feeble-mindedness; Its Causes and Consequences", Goddard, The Macmillan Company.

[519] **The After-Treatment of Pneumonia** is important, and every detail has a distinct bearing on the ultimate recovery and establishment of good health. Careful feeding, a good tonic, and the proper attention to exercise, fresh air and bathing are requisite. A change of air after the fever is gone is more important than all other measures put together. A dry, warm

climate where patients can be kept in the open air is preferable. The danger of allowing a slow, long drawn-out convalescence after pneumonia is the development of tuberculosis.

ADENOIDS

Adenoids are very common, almost popular, in childhood. The condition is one that causes more real trouble and discomfort than any other childhood affliction. Adenoids are associated with, and are responsible for, many of the ailments of childhood. They may be associated with enlarged tonsils or they may be independent of them. They may be present at birth or develop any time thereafter, though they are more frequent between the ages of two and six years. Children who have adenoids invariably suffer from chronic "head-colds" with a discharge from the nose. These chronic colds are caused by the adenoids. Nearly every disease, and every diseased, or abnormal, condition of the nose, throat, larynx, and lungs can be directly caused by the presence of adenoids. They are also responsible for numerous other conditions of very grave importance in the growing child. The accompanying "head-colds" may develop into a bronchitis which may keep the child indoors for a long period. Adenoids always interfere with respiration, thereby depriving the child of a normal quantity of oxygen, thus rendering the blood less pure, and, as a consequence, seriously interfering with the nourishment and general health. The impaired nourishment and poor health thus produced, as a direct result of adenoids, renders the child more liable to disease; he may thus acquire ailments that may affect his whole subsequent life. The mental side of a child's development is also affected by the presence of adenoids, so much so that actual statistics prove that these children cannot keep up with their classes in the public school. [520]

We must therefore regard the presence of adenoids as a serious menace to the health and comfort of the patient. It has already been pointed out in discussing other diseases that before a cure of these diseases could be permanently accomplished it would be absolutely necessary to remove the adenoids, which were, no doubt, the actual cause, or an important contributing cause, of the disease. Such conditions as catarrhal laryngitis, croup, chronic recurring winter coughs, acute catarrhal rhinitis, "snuffles", "cold in the head", chronic catarrh, bronchial asthma, incontinence of urine, "bed-wetting", "nose-bleeding", headaches in growing children, anemia, deafness, night terrors, defective speech, diphtheria, consumption, are frequently caused by the presence of adenoids.

These patients contract certain diseases easier than other children, and when they do, they have them more severely; such diseases are diphtheria, tuberculosis, scarlet fever, measles, and whooping cough.

Adenoid children are, as a rule, in better health during the warm, equable, summer weather than during the changeable, uncertain weather we have in the winter months. If the case is neglected, and if the adenoids have existed for a long time, the growth of the child is impaired. He remains small and stunted, and the expression of the face is dull and stupid. The temperament and disposition are affected also; such children are languid, listless and depressed.

How to Tell When a Child Has Adenoids.—Children with well-developed adenoids are "mouth-breathers." Instead of breathing through the nose they breathe with the mouth open, especially when sound asleep. If a child has a discharge from its nose and a chronic cough, both of which resist treatment, and if in addition it is a mouth-breather, it is safe to investigate the naso-pharynx for adenoids. If a child with these symptoms is not in good health, is listless and depressed, looks stupid, snores at night, has difficulty in breathing and cannot blow its nose satisfactorily, is troubled occasionally with "nose bleeds" and headaches, we may be satisfied that the child has adenoids, as no other condition could produce such a picture.[521]

Adenoids, like enlarged tonsils, are dangerous, apart from the physical distress and disease which they cause, owing to the fact that they harbor deadly bacteria, and from these bacteria, which find a lodgment in the adenoids and tonsils, a fatal attack of diphtheria or consumption may have its beginning.

Treatment of Adenoids.—Absolute removal is the only justifiable treatment. This is rendered imperative for so many reasons that it is unnecessary to go into details in justification of the procedure.

The physical well-being, the mental development, the life of the child depend upon it. Any parent who would wittingly interpose an objection to the removal of his or her child's adenoids, after they have been demonstrated to exist, would be guilty of a grave crime.

The operation itself is not at all dangerous. It is over in a few moments and the child is well in an hour or two, so far as any pain or suffering is concerned.

Physicians are frequently asked if adenoids "grow" again after removal. The answer is, "Yes," they sometimes do. In a very small percentage of the cases they do return. The older the child is when they are removed the less chance there is of a recurrence. A child operated on before it is two years of age is more liable to a recurrence than a child operated on at six years of age. This must not, however, be construed as an excuse for putting an operation off, because if a child needs an operation at two years and it is postponed till later, its health will be permanently injured before it is four years of age.

SUMMARY:—

1. Adenoids cause more trouble and more actual disease than any other condition during childhood.

2. It is a crime for a parent to refuse operation if the presence of adenoids has been proved.

3. Removal is the only treatment and it should be done in every case as soon as possible.

4. The operation is a trivial one and is free from danger.

[522]

NASAL HEMORRHAGE—"NOSE BLEEDS"

A hemorrhage from the nose may occur at any time from birth on. It depends upon the rupture of one or more blood vessels. The great majority of "nose-bleeds" are caused by adenoids, or by a small ulcer in the nose, or by an injury, such as a blow or fall. A nasal hemorrhage, however, may be caused by other, more serious conditions, and for that reason may justify a careful inquiry into the cause, especially if bleeding should occur a number of times, or be of a serious character the first time.

Of the more common causes as given above, the adenoids should be removed, and the chronic catarrh which is invariably the cause of the ulcer should be cured.

Treatment of an Acute Attack.—Have the patient sit erect; loosen all tight clothing around neck; fold the hands over the head; apply cold to the back of the neck and the nose. Pieces of ice can be put into the nostril and the ice bag to the nape of the neck, or a piece of ice can be put into a folded napkin and held on the back of the neck. Taking a long breath and holding it as long as possible and repeating it while the ice is being applied is an aid. Placing the feet in hot mustard water is of decided use. Another excellent expedient is to wrap absorbent cotton round a smooth probe (piece of whalebone, for example), dip the cotton in an alum-water mixture (half teaspoonful powdered alum in a half cupful of water), and then push it into the bleeding nostril as far as you can with gentle force. A valuable remedy is Peroxide of Hydrogen used full strength and freely dropped into the nostril. If these measures fail, send for a physician at once.

SUMMARY:—

1st. Nose bleeds may be caused by some serious condition.

2nd. If they occur a number of times have the child examined.

3rd. If the treatment outlined above does not stop the bleeding in a few moments send immediately for a physician.

[523]

QUINSY

Quinsy is not common in childhood. It usually follows tonsilitis when it is seen. The child complains of pain in the neck, extreme pain and difficulty upon swallowing, and inability to open the mouth as much as usual. There is a tendency to hold the head to one side. The treatment is to open the abscess at the earliest moment after pus is present.

HICCOUGH

Hiccough is, in most cases, in infancy and childhood caused by some irritation of the stomach, may be over-filled with food or gas. In these cases it is an unimportant incident and may be quickly relieved by giving the child an enema of soap-water and a laxative of rhubarb and soda.

Infrequently hiccough may be the result of cold feet, or a surface chill. Simple methods of relief are, to hold the breath, to expire, or blow the breath out as long as possible before taking the next breath; to sip water from a cup held by another person while the tips of the two fore-fingers are in the ears.

Hiccough is quite frequent in hysteria in girls, but it is of no consequence. When hiccoughs set in during the course of any serious disease it is a very unfavorable sign.

SORE MOUTH: STOMATITIS

Stomatitis is an inflammation of the mucous membrane (inner lining) of the mouth. The gums and the inner surface of the lips and cheeks may be red and angry-looking. There may be small grayish spots on any part of the mouth. If the case is very bad or if it has lasted some time and has been neglected, these spots grow larger and join together forming irregular grayish plaques. A large percentage of the cases never go further than this because the proper care and attention is given them. It is possible, however, for any case to progress further and become ulcerative. This will be [524] observed first as a faint yellow line at the margin of the teeth and gum. Ulceration never takes place unless the child has teeth. The quantity of saliva is very greatly increased, so much so that it flows out of the mouth soiling the clothes. The saliva is intensely acid and it consequently irritates the skin, causing more or less eczema. The mouth is painful and hot. There is slight fever, but seldom any marked prostration. If, however, the ulceration should be severe, the fever may be quite high.

There is one feature of these cases that sometimes proves vexatious and annoying. Because of the soreness of the mouth, the child cannot draw strongly enough on the nipple to get a normal feeding, and as a result the nutrition of the child is poor. These children are hungry and when offered the nipple grasp it greedily, draw a few mouthfuls then stop because of the pain and begin to cry.

If the ulceration is extensive, there is usually an odor and the gums bleed easily. Sometimes the teeth fall out or have to be drawn out.

Strong, well-fed children are as likely to develop stomatitis as are those who are weakly and ill fed.

The disease is caused by infection and is contagious. Just what the infection is we do not know; we do, however, know that children whose mouths are carefully cleaned after each feeding do not have sore mouths of this character. When cleaning the mouth care must be observed not to injure the tender mucous membrane.

Treatment.—As soon as the condition is observed mouth-washing should be systematically and thoroughly carried out. After each feeding the mouth should be washed with a saturated solution of boric acid in boiled water. (See page 626.)

It is not necessary to use any further treatment, as a rule. Patients recover in four to eight days. Strict attention to cleanliness, however, is imperative. The feeding bottle and nipple, or the mother's nipple, if breast fed, must be kept scrupulously clean.

The feeding of these children is sometimes a problem for a day or two, because, as stated above, of the soreness of the mouth. This is best overcome by feeding the baby with a spoon. If breast fed, it is necessary to pump the [525] milk and then feed with the spoon. Children will take the milk better if it is fed cold. Cold boiled water is largely taken and is good for them at this time.

Treatment for Ulcers in Mouth.—The ulcers should be touched with a camel's-hair brush which has been dipped into finely powdered burnt alum. If a stronger caustic is necessary, the solid stick of nitrate of silver may be used.

A mouth wash may also be used in the ulcerative cases, composed of the peroxide of hydrogen diluted with two parts of water. If this is used wash the mouth out afterward with plain, cool, boiled water. The peroxide mouth wash can be used four or five times daily.

In addition to the mouth washing in the ulcerative cases it is advisable to use internally chlorate of potash. The druggist should be requested to make a two-ounce saturated solution, and of this you can give one-half teaspoonful, largely diluted with cool water, every hour during the day for the first twenty-four hours, then every two hours until marked improvement is shown, when it can be further reduced by lengthening the interval between doses.

SPRUE—THRUSH

Sprue is a form of sore mouth. It is seen only during the first six months of life, as a rule. It affects the mucous membrane of the mouth; it appears in the form of small white spots that look like drops of curdled milk. They are on the inner surface of the cheek and may be all over the mouth, and on the tongue. The spots are firmly attached, and if forcibly removed the mucous membrane will bleed.

The disease is caused by infection through lack of cleanliness and it invariably affects poorly nourished children, especially those who are bottle-fed.

There are no symptoms other than those of the mouth; the child frequently refuses to nurse because of evident pain and distress while nursing. The condition is not contagious. It may be cured in from six to eight days without difficulty.

Treatment.—Mouth irrigations of boracic acid are all [526] that are necessary. They are given in the following way: Place the child on its side, roll around the index finger a piece of absorbent cotton, dip this in a saturated solution of boracic acid, and put into the mouth of the child. Let the cotton take up as much of the solution as it will hold, so that when it is lightly pressed on the tongue and cheeks it will flow out of the mouth, thus "irrigating the mouth." Repeat this a number of times, pressing the cotton to a different part each time. This should be gone through from four to six times daily.

If the child is a bottle-fed baby, care should be taken in cleaning the nipples and bottles as directed on page 264. If the patient is breast-fed, care must be taken to note that the mother's nipples are clean. They should be washed with the same solution of boracic acid and not handled. If the child cannot nurse it is necessary to feed it with a spoon.

In obstinate cases the parts may be touched with a one per cent. solution of formalin. Mothers should particularly note not to use honey and borax, as is often recommended by women who know no better, in any disease of the mouth in children. [527]

CHAPTER XXXV

DISEASES OF THE STOMACH AND GASTRO-INTESTINAL CANAL

Inflammation of the Stomach—Acute Gastritis— Persistent Vomiting—Acute Gastric Indigestion—Iced Champagne in Persistent Vomiting—Acute Intestinal Diseases of Children— Conditions Under Which They Exist and Suggestions as to Remedial Measures—Acute Intestinal Indigestion— Symptoms of Acute Intestinal Indigestion—Treatment of Acute Intestinal Indigestion—Children with Whom Milk Does Not Agree—Chronic or Persistent Intestinal Indigestion —Acute Ileo-colitis—Dysentery— Enteritis— Entero-colitis—Inflammatory Diarrhea—Chronic Ileo-colitis —Chronic Colitis—Summer Diarrhea—Cholera Infantum— Gastro-enteritis—Acute Gastro-enteric Infection—Gastro-enteric Intoxication—Colic Appendicitis—Jaundice in Infants—Jaundice in Older Children—Catarrhal Jaundice—Gastro-duodenitis—Intestinal Worms—Worms, Thread, Pin and Tape—Rupture

ACUTE GASTRIC INDIGESTION

Acute Inflammation of the Stomach—Acute Gastritis— Persistent Vomiting

An infant seldom has real inflammation of the stomach. Gastric, or stomach, indigestion is the better name, because it actually signifies the true condition. It is indigestion that causes a child to vomit, though it is possible to have a true inflammation caused by the taking of irritant or corrosive drugs.

Gastric indigestion causes sudden, repeated vomiting, with prostration and occasional fever. It is caused by unsuitable food, the wrong quantity of food, irregular feeding, and food the quality of which is not good.

Treatment.—The stomach should be immediately washed out. Until the physician arrives the mother can encourage the child to drink a large quantity of cool boiled water. This will be vomited and it will wash out the stomach at the same time. No further treatment [528] may be necessary, as the vomiting may stop. All food should be withheld for at least twenty-four hours. A high rectal irrigation should now be given. It is essential to know that the bowel is absolutely clean in all vomiting cases. The normal salt solution is the best agent to use for a high enema in infants. (See page 586.)

After twelve or twenty-four hours' abstinence from food, the child can be given teaspoonful doses every twenty minutes of cooled boiled water, or barley or albumen water, weak tea, or chicken broth. Cold liquids are better retained and more readily taken than those that are heated. If the liquid feedings are vomited, another twelve hours must elapse before trying stomach feedings. In these cases we must try to satisfy the thirst by giving cold colon flushings. If the case becomes protracted and we find it impossible to nourish the child by the mouth, we must wash the stomach out once every day with a five per cent. solution of bicarbonate of soda, and feed the child by the rectum. Sometimes we can feed through the stomach tube. Liquids will frequently be retained when put into the stomach through a tube when they will be vomited if swallowed.

The best food by the rectum is plain peptonized milk.

Drugs are absolutely useless. If the vomiting persists, despite the above efforts to stop it, there is nothing to be gained by experimenting. You will not only render the condition worse but you will weaken the child. Morphine given hypodermatically is the only remedy. Given in appropriate doses, according to age, it is absolutely harmless. It will not only stop the vomiting, but it will give the child a much-needed rest, by allowing it to go to sleep. When it wakes up it will be stronger and its stomach will most likely retain small doses of nourishment.

Great care must be exercised, in getting the child back on a normal diet, not to try to go too fast.

In cases of persistent vomiting in children I have found it advisable to use teaspoonful doses of ice-cold champagne. These children will sometimes keep this down when all other liquids will be vomited. It is absolutely necessary to keep the child lying down. If he is [529] restless or sits up, the vomiting may begin all over again. The champagne not only is excellent nourishment for the child, but it quiets the stomach, allays irritability, and frequently favors sleep, during which time a cure very often results. The champagne must be drawn through a champagne siphon (procured in the drug store), and the bottle must be kept on ice with the mouth downward; otherwise it will get stale very quickly and be of no use. If kept as advised it will remain good to the end.

SUMMARY:—

1st. Persistent vomiting in a child means acute gastritis. Stop all food for twenty-four hours.

2nd. Encourage the child to drink large quantities of slightly warm water; this will wash the stomach out and frequently stops the vomiting.

3rd. When the child is quiet wash out the bowels.

4th. If vomiting persists, use iced champagne as directed.

ACUTE INTESTINAL DISEASES OF CHILDREN

The large infant mortality that results from intestinal diseases during the summer months is deserving of the most careful consideration, both of the physician and the parent.

Apart from the excessive heat of the summer, there is no doubt that an unfavorable environment, which means bad hygienic surroundings, bad sanitary conditions, bad food and home influences, contributes largely to the enormous number of these serious cases. Education, while it may be expected to influence favorably the sanitary and other conditions in the home, cannot change the home location. The child must continue to live in the same environment. It is in this class of cases that these summer diseases are so very fatal. Children in better circumstances can take advantage of conditions which are denied to the tenement child. The diseases must therefore be faced and treated under these existing conditions. [530]

In addition to the climate and the environment, there are certain factors that occur in all classes which result in intestinal derangement. If the stomach or bowels are not performing their function properly, or if the food or method of feeding is wrong, these, plus very hot, humid weather, invariably result in serious intestinal disease. The mother must be taught to interpret properly the meaning of a green, loose stool in the summertime; she must appreciate that it is the danger signal and must be regarded seriously.

The very best preventive against summer diseases of the intestine is to guard particularly against any trouble with the child's stomach at all seasons of the year. A healthy stomach and bowel will resist disease, even in very hot weather.

The most important food product which has a direct relationship to this class of diseases is milk. In a large city like New York it will remain impossible to solve the milk problem, despite the splendid efforts of the Health Department and the members of the medical profession, until the city itself shall establish milk depots and ice stations where safe milk, and ice to keep it safe, may be obtained at a nominal cost, or free, if the parents cannot afford to buy it. We, therefore, must recognize that the vast majority of children to-day are taking milk that is not suited to them, that is really not fit as a food for children. The mothers do not know this and no steps are taken to render the milk more safe for them to feed to their children. These mothers are willing to do what is essential in the interest of their children, but they do not know what should be done. These people cannot afford a physician or a nurse to teach them, nor do they even know that their methods are wrong or that they need any instruction. We must carry the information and the explanation to them. We must show them the need for a change of methods. This is the work for those charitably disposed women who desire some worthy purpose in life, who really wish to do some real good. All the equipment they need is good common sense. They will tell these mothers why it is necessary to pasteurize the milk before feeding it to the baby. They [531] will show how to keep the nursing bottles clean, and the nipples sweet and fresh. They will instruct them how to dress the baby in the hot weather and impress them with the need of giving it all the cool, fresh air possible. In short, they will gain the confidence and the good will of these mothers in a tactful and diplomatic way, and they will tell them all they know in language which they will understand regarding the care of the baby. In every city in the country this work is needed and is waiting for the missionaries who will volunteer. To teach mothers the need for boiled water as a necessary drink for baby and older children is alone a worthy avocation. To impress upon one of these willing but ignorant mothers the absolute necessity for washing her hands before she prepares her baby's food, that she must keep a covered vessel in which the soiled napkins are placed until washed, that she should frequently sponge her baby in the hot weather, and explain thoroughly why these are important details, is a work of true religious charity. They should be specially taught to immediately discontinue milk at the first sign of intestinal trouble, to give a suitable dose of castor oil and to put the child on barley water as a food until the danger is passed. They should be taught to know the significance of a green, watery stool, they should know that is the one danger signal in the summer time that no mother can ignore without wilfully risking the life of her baby. They should be taught to prepare special articles of diet when they are needed. If every mother were educated to the extent as indicated in the above outline the appalling infant mortality would fall into insignificance. It is not a difficult task nor would it take a long time to carry it out; it is the work for willing women who have time and who perhaps spend that time in less desirable but more dramatic ways.

It is the knowledge that aids in catching disease in its inception that counts. The worst infections begin as a mild condition and prompt treatment robs them of their sting. When treatment is delayed and the child is fed for twenty-four hours too long on milk, the condition which in the beginning could have been stopped promptly has developed and it becomes a fight for life.
[532]

It will be seen from the above that all we need is education. Education of the mother primarily, but education of the missionary, the nurse, the physician, the municipality, and the State, each co-operating, each willing to work in the interest of a great cause, for the benefit of the human race and for the brotherhood of man.

ACUTE INTESTINAL INDIGESTION

Causes.—Overfeeding, unsuitable and improper food, irregular and indiscriminate feeding, sudden change from one food to another, as at weaning time, a change from a poor quality to a rich food, or vice versa. Conditions affecting the health of the child, especially the nervous system, such as hot weather, extreme cold, fatigue, or at the beginning of any of the acute diseases. Children sometimes are predisposed to attacks of intestinal indigestion; these children are delicate in health and have weak digestive ability. The slightest irregularity or error in diet will cause an attack in these children.

Symptoms.—The attack may come on suddenly or it may develop slowly. The important constitutional symptoms are fever, prostration, and a general nervous irritability. The child is seized with pain in the abdomen. The pain is referred to the region around the navel. It is sharp, colicky, and severe, causing the child to cry out and draw up its legs in an effort to lessen its severity. The child is exceedingly restless and acts as if it were on the verge of a dangerous illness. Gas in the bowel is not present as a rule as frequently as it is in infants under the same circumstances. In a few hours diarrhea sets in, the stools may number from four to twelve or more in twenty-four hours. The stools are acid, sour, and the odor may be very foul. They are thinner than usual and frothy from the presence of gas.

In very young infants suffering from a sudden attack of intestinal indigestion, the stomach, as well as the bowels, is invariably upset. If the indigestion is the result of a slower process, the stomach does not participate in the process. The color of the stools in infancy is yellow, then yellowish-green, and later grass-green. [533] Undigested food is always present and in infants the curdled casein of the milk appears as white specks or lumps in the movements.

The fever is high in the sudden cases and lower in the cases of gradual onset. The prostration is more severe when the onset is sudden and in infants may be very marked.

The termination of the disease depends upon the cause, the treatment, and the previous health of the child. In healthy children promptly and properly treated it may be all over in a week. In delicate, poorly nourished children, and especially in the summer time, it may be the beginning of trouble that may eventuate in death.

Treatment.—There is no condition in the whole realm of diseases of childhood where the knowledge of the mother may have such important results as this condition. The most effective time to treat these cases of intestinal indigestion is before the physician is called. There are few diseases in which time is so valuable, so far as final results are concerned, as it is here. Every mother should know the significance of a loose, green stool. She should be taught that it means danger and consequently demands prompt treatment. The first indication is to empty, thoroughly, the bowel. The best means for this purpose, if it is immediately procurable, is calomel. If calomel is not procurable at once give castor oil, two teaspoonfuls to an infant, one tablespoonful to an older child. Calomel should be given in one-eighth-grain doses, repeated every three-quarters of an hour for eight or twelve doses, until the bowel is thoroughly cleaned out. Don't be afraid of a few extra movements at the beginning. Better clean out thoroughly at the start than to be compelled to do it all over again after the child is weak and suffering from the poison of the disease. The next important thing to do is to stop milk at once. The thirst is usually intense and if vomiting is not present it can be moderately relieved by giving small quantities frequently of cool boiled water or mineral water or strained albumen or barley water. We quite often have to stop all food and liquids by the mouth for twenty-four hours. [534]

If the prostration is very great and the child looks as though it might collapse, it can be given brandy in cracked ice from time to time.

After the bowels have been thoroughly cleaned out, never before, some medicinal agent may be given to stop the unnecessary diarrhea. In a very large number of promptly and properly treated cases this is not needed. If it is thought best to use it the physician will select the agent according to the conditions present and prescribe it.

Breast-fed infants rarely have intestinal diseases of a severe type. If they should develop diarrhea they must be taken off the mother's milk for twenty-four hours. They should be given a dose of castor oil or calomel and fed on barley water in the interval. The feedings should be reduced in quantity and the interval doubled. The two-hour interval will become a four-hour feeding: the three or four ounces at each feeding can be reduced to two ounces. The intention is to simply give as little as possible while the diarrhea is under way.

The mother's breasts must be pumped at the regular feeding time in order to preserve the flow, release the pressure, and keep the milk fresh.

It is sometimes a problem to renew feedings of milk without exciting a relapse of the diarrhea. It should not be tried until the stools are normal in color and consistency. This may not be for three or four days. In resuming the milk it should be given in smaller amounts and diluted with lime water or barley water for the first day. Gruels may be given to which skimmed milk may be added: later add the ordinary milk. If it is well digested and does not cause any return of the diarrhea, the quantity of milk can be slowly increased until the former feedings are resumed. It is often of very great advantage to boil the milk for some time. Peptonized milk is safe and can be used in bottle-fed infants after diarrhea. In older children, meat, broths, eggs, boiled milk, and dry toast bread may be used sparingly for some time. Cereals, vegetables, fruits, should be withheld for a considerable time and watched carefully when resumed. Kumyss, buttermilk, matzoon, bacillac, and [535] other fermented milks are better borne than plain milk. All of these children need rest, fresh air, change of air, frequent bathing, and tonics, as an attack of this kind leaves them depressed, weak, languid, and anemic.

SUMMARY:—

1st. When a child complains of sharp, colicky, severe pains in the abdomen, around navel, which are shortly followed by foul, sour, frothy diarrhea,—greenish in color, it has acute intestinal indigestion.

2nd. Every mother should know that a green stool means danger. She should know to give at once a cathartic,—castor oil is good, but give a good large dose—then stop all food for twenty-four hours. If she learns this lesson she will have time to wait for the doctor; meantime, she may have saved her child's life.

CHILDREN WITH WHOM MILK DOES NOT AGREE

Contrary to the general belief, there are quite a large number of children in whom milk seems to act as a poison. These children are not necessarily constipated. They suffer, however, from a slow, continuous intestinal toxemia or poison. The symptoms of this condition are headache, disorders of speech, habitual sleep-talking, sleep-walking, and general nervous irritability without cause: they are listless, languid, and constantly tired. They may be bright in the morning and sleepy in the afternoon. They are irritable and cross and touchy.

Treatment.—Milk must be wholly discontinued. Eggs must be restricted to one every second day, and meat but once daily. The use of green vegetables is particularly suitable and should be given daily. Cereals and fruit also are good. Malted milk, kumyss, or matzoon may be given in place of milk. If constipation is present, rhubarb and soda mixture is an excellent laxative in these cases. A tonic should be prescribed for all these children.

DYSENTERY—ENTERITIS—ENTERO-COLITIS—INFLAMMATORY DIARRHEA

Cause.—Any cause which has been mentioned as a [536] cause of ordinary diarrhea may result in this disease. It may occur at any time of the year and at any age. It may follow the infectious diseases. It may follow any other disease of the intestines.

Symptoms.—It may begin like an ordinary attack of acute intestinal indigestion. There is usually vomiting, fever, pain, and frequent yellow or green stools. The passages may be blood-stained and there may be little or much mucus. The stools at the beginning have no odor as a rule. The bowels move very frequently, often with little or nothing to pass. There may be pain with each movement. The blood may disappear in a few days, but the mucus remains, often in large quantity in each stool.

At the beginning the fever is high, but it soon falls and remains low during the attack. The child loses weight, is irritable, has no appetite, and looks and acts sick. When the attack is over these children do not gain their strength as readily as we would like; recovery is slow.

The acute symptoms usually last about one week, after this time the child begins to recover, but the process is a tedious one and one in which much care has to be exercised. It is an encouraging sign to note the disappearance of the blood in the stools and the return of the movements to the normal brown color. When these favorable signs are wanting the bowel is probably ulcerated and it will take a much longer time to return to normal and to be free from blood and mucus.

The above is the ordinary form of this disease and it ends in recovery as a rule. There is a more severe form, however, which differs from the above in the following way:

The fever is high and remains high; the stools are more frequent and there is more blood and more mucus in them; the child is much more irritable and is more profoundly sick. Death may occur at any time from the second day. If the little patient survives, the return to health is a very slow process; it often takes months and frequently years before a reasonable degree of strength is regained. Relapses are common, and they [537] are very difficult to treat and care for. In some cases the child never wholly regains its former strength.

There are children who have been the victims of other intestinal diseases or conditions who develop colitis. The colitis in these cases may come on suddenly with vomiting and high fever, or it begins slowly, with no vomiting and with little fever. Their appetite is poor, their digestion is feeble, their prostration is pronounced. They lose flesh rapidly and may be emaciated to a remarkable degree. Very few of these cases recover completely. Serious and sometimes fatal relapses may take place. The feeding of these children is a difficult task and the greatest care must be constantly taken; a very little mistake may cost the life of the child.

Treatment.—All diseases of the intestine in childhood should be promptly and efficiently treated. If any form of diarrhea is neglected, it may result in the development of ileo-colitis with all its risks and uncertainty. When a child is seized with sudden bowel trouble, no matter what variety it is, it should be treated with the greatest care because "sudden" bowel trouble usually means plenty of trouble if it is neglected.

Fresh air is essential in all these cases. A change of air is of decided value as soon as the immediate symptoms have abated. The diet is the same as for children who have gastro-enteric intoxication. Later, much difficulty will be met because these patients have absolutely no appetite,—peptonized skimmed milk is always good, beef broths are often well borne, liquid beef peptonoids may be tried. The food should be given every three hours. Boiled water and stimulants may be given between the feedings. Later in older children, raw beef, eggs, boiled milk, kumyss, or matzoon and gruels may be given. Great care has to be taken for months after an attack; relapses may be caused by changes of temperature, by fatigue, and, of course, by improper feeding. These children should avoid potatoes, tomatoes, fruits, corn, oatmeal, and a great many other things which an intelligent mother would not give any sick child, as candy, cakes, pastries, etc.

Cases which begin with free vomiting, thin stools; [538] and fever should be treated at once. The bowels must be thoroughly cleaned out, the colon should be thoroughly irrigated, and all food should be stopped. When there are bloody stools with mucus and pain we must depend upon castor oil, irrigations of the colon, and opium and bismuth by the mouth. A good big dose of oil at the beginning is always necessary. If, however, the stomach is irritable and will not tolerate castor oil, we may substitute calomel in one-fourth-grain doses every hour for six doses, to be followed by citrate of magnesium. Irrigation of the colon in these cases is one of the essential means of successful treatment; it should be done twice a day during the first few days of the disease.

Stimulants are needed in all the cases. They help the heart, act as a food, and tend to quiet the general nervousness by favoring sleep. Good brandy given in boiled cool water is the best stimulant.

After the child is over the worst of the acute symptoms all medicine should be withdrawn and the proper kind of food given. Tonics will aid in restoring the strength. Cod Liver Oil during the following winter is a very good plan to aid in building up the vitality of the weakened bowel, but it must not be given too soon.

CHRONIC ILEO-COLITIS—CHRONIC COLITIS

Chronic Ileo-colitis fellows the acute variety. Cases which are unusually severe or which have been badly managed are likely to become chronic. A child suffering from this disease presents the following picture: The patient is emaciated, the abdomen is usually enlarged with gas, the feet are cold, the circulation of the blood is poor, the fever is low or absent altogether except when the child is having a relapse, when it jumps up suddenly. The bowels are loose and contain mucus, frequently in large quantities. The mucus may stop for a few days; then it appears again with a rise of temperature accompanied with loose stools with foul odor. These children are exceedingly nervous and irritable and are very poor sleepers. [539]

Parents should be told it will be impossible to effect a rapid cure of these cases. It often takes months to get them started on the safe road. The slightest mistake or change in the weather will upset the progress of the cure and it will be necessary to begin all over again. The entire hope of cure rests with the mother. She must be faithful, patient, and must carry out the physician's instructions implicitly. The management consists in diet, change of climate, and such other treatment as the physician finds necessary in each individual case.

Treatment.—In children under one year of age the only hope is breast milk, which must be given in small quantities. They do not do well on any starch food for a considerable period.

Where breast milk is not available the whites of two or three eggs may be given daily. They may be beaten up and given in skimmed milk, or in plain water with a little salt added. Zwieback or bread crumbs may be given in small quantities. They should be fed at four-hour intervals.

Older children may take skimmed milk, raw scraped beef, junket, and coddled white of egg or raw egg, bread crumbs, toasted, or zwieback.

A rectal enema must be given every twenty-four hours if the bowels have not moved. If constipation is the habit a laxative should be given; the aromatic fluid extract of cascara sagrada or magnesia are suitable. At least one free movement every day is essential to success.

Colon irrigations are only to be used when there is a rise of temperature, irrespective of whether the bowels have moved or not.

When convalescence is established these children should be given a maximum of fresh air and should be treated as recommended in cases of malnutrition.

SUMMER DIARRHEA

As the name implies, this is the form of diarrhea that is so common, especially in cities, in summer. It is always preceded by some milder condition which paves the way for the more serious diarrhea. Acute [540] indigestion is, as a general rule, the forerunner of cholera infantum. The influence of hot weather must always be kept in mind as the underlying factor which no doubt conduces to gastro-intestinal disease of infancy and childhood. The depression incident to a spell of hot and possibly humid weather tends to interfere with the digestive process of babies and children. When this function is carried on imperfectly, the strength and vitality of the child fails, and if immediate steps are not taken to check the process, diarrhea makes its appearance. If these children are improperly fed, or if their surroundings are not sanitary; if they are not getting fresh air enough, or if they suffer because of lack of attention, and have at the same time a little indigestion, it is only a step further to develop a full-fledged cholera infantum.

The outcome of any case of summer diarrhea is questionable. It is not safe to make any promise. An apparently mild attack may prove quickly fatal. Much depends upon the previous history of the child. If it has been a strong, healthy child it has a very good chance if treated energetically and correctly. If it has previously suffered from bad nutrition, is not robust, has had trouble with its stomach, etc., the chances are against it.

The one lesson to be learned by all mothers is, as stated above, to act quickly; to be on the watch all through the summer months for any trouble with the baby's stomach or bowels. It is much easier to treat and cure a little trouble than to battle against an established gastro-enteric intoxication. Overfeeding and indiscriminate feeding must be religiously avoided,—they are the two most prolific causes of stomach and intestinal troubles in childhood.

Symptoms.—The onset is sudden and pronounced. The child begins to vomit and continues vomiting and retching persistently. The bowels are loose, and large, watery, greenish stools are frequent. The prostration is very marked, the child looks seriously sick, respiration is quick and shallow, the eyes sunken, the skin becomes ashen gray in color, and the pulse is soft and very [541] rapid. The fever may be very high or it may remain low. The low febrile cases are the worst.

If taken in hand quickly and if the treatment is energetic and if the child reacts, the case may go rapidly on to recovery and the child be wholly well in a few days; or it may not react, but be overwhelmed by the poison and sink and die in twenty-four hours.

Treatment.—In the treatment of cholera infantum it must not be forgotten that the dangerous element is the poisoning of the system that is constantly going on. It is difficult for the non-medical mind to estimate the importance of this element. It is, of course, caused by the bacteria present in the gastro-intestinal canal. There are numberless millions of bacteria in the normal healthy bowel. A very large percentage of those germs are good for us, are there for a beneficent purpose, and can and do protect us from other germs which occasionally find their way into the bowel and whose purpose is not a peaceful one. When the bowel condition changes, as during an attack of summer diarrhea, it is invaded by multitudes of evil-intentioned germs. These germs find conditions in the diseased bowel exceedingly favorable to them, so they begin work in an active, energetic way. The result of their activity is highly poisonous, and, as the good germs are virtually out of business and are consequently not working in our interest, we are absolutely in the hands of the enemy. There is soon manufactured, by these invading germs, enough poison to poison the entire system of the child. It is this feature that we must combat in summer diarrhea.

It is absolutely essential to keep these cases as much in the open fresh air as possible. No matter how sick they may be, this rule must be observed. Light clothing is advisable.

If it is a city child that is affected and it does not show decided improvement in three or four days, it should, if possible, be sent to the country. There is always distinct danger of a relapse in every case, so the little victim should be given a change of air as soon as convalescence permits. The seashore is preferable to the mountains in all intestinal cases. [542]

In the care of these patients cleanliness is an important factor and counts much in the ultimate cure. The child, as well as the clothing, should be kept scrupulously clean. Napkins as soon as soiled should be removed and put into a disinfecting solution. The buttocks should be well powdered after each movement to prevent sores developing.

Feeding must be stopped at once. No food of any kind should be given for at least twenty-four hours, or until the tendency to vomit subsides. The thirst must be allayed, however, so we give frequently small quantities of thin barley water or albumen water or cold boiled water. If these are vomited we must stop giving them altogether for twenty-four hours. If the fever is high and the skin dry, the child should be given a cool pack, 85° to 90° F., which can be moistened every half hour with water at this temperature; this will often control the fever satisfactorily. Hot-water bottles should be placed at the feet if they are cold.

If, on the other hand, the fever is very low (below normal), the child's circulation poor, the skin blue and cold, a hot-water bath at 108° F., for five minutes (rubbing the surface of the body while in the bath), will be of very great service. The bath may be repeated at half-hour intervals.

If the patient is a breast-fed infant it can be allowed to nurse after the twenty-four-hour rest. The length of time it is permitted to stay at the breast should be about one-quarter of the time it was allowed before the attack began. If it does not vomit, the nursing can be repeated every four hours. As the case progresses toward recovery the interval between feedings can be shortened. Care, however, must be taken not to shorten the interval too rapidly.

If the patient is artificially fed and is not over four months old, a substitute for the milk must be found. The best substitutes are rice or barley water, either plain or dextrinized, the malted foods, chicken or beef broths, liquid peptonoids or bovinine. Water (boiled and cooled) may be allowed at all times if not vomited.

Older children are treated in the same way. All food [543] is withheld while there is any vomiting. When vomiting stops begin with small quantities of beef broth, or chicken, or veal broth. Later kumyss or matzoon can be tried, and finally thin gruels made with milk.

If vomiting persists the stomach must be washed out; this can be done by giving the infant or child a large drink of cool boiled water. This will be immediately vomited and it will clean the stomach at the same time. The stomach-pump may be used to better advantage. One washing is usually sufficient. The vomiting will stop after the stomach has been washed out and the patient may then be given, frequently, small quantities of cold albumen water or barley water.

The bowel should be thoroughly cleaned out at the beginning of every summer diarrhea. Castor oil or calomel are the two best cathartics for this purpose. If the stomach is not upset use castor oil. If the stomach is upset use calomel; one-fourth of a grain every hour for eight doses will be sufficient. Give enough, however,—there is no danger at the beginning of the attack of too free movements of the bowel. Whatever cathartic is given, it should produce green, watery stools.

Irrigation of the bowel is an exceedingly effective way of cleaning out the poison-laden large intestine. It should be done in every instance unless the movements are watery and of such frequency as to render irrigation unnecessary. Once or twice daily will be sufficient in even the worst cases. The irrigation should be given at the temperature of 100° F, and should be the normal saline solution; a long rectal tube is used to give the irrigation.

SUMMARY:—

1st. Cholera infantum is one of the most dangerous, one of the most treacherous, and one of the quickest acting diseases of childhood.

2nd. Don't temporize, don't delay, don't regard lightly any diarrhea during the summer time.

3rd. Give a large dose of castor oil and withhold all nourishment until the doctor sees the little [544] patient in every case of diarrhea during the warm weather.

4th. Keep the child in a cool, quiet place and don't handle or annoy it.

5th. Follow, your doctor's directions implicitly. The fight may be short, sharp, and decisive. Don't pave the way for regrets afterward. Do everything while you have the chance.

COLIC

Colic is a common condition in infancy. Very few children escape more or less colic during the first few months of life. It does not seem to injure permanently some infants; they go on growing according to standard, eat and sleep, and seem contented and happy despite occasional severe attacks of colic. Other children suffer seriously; the degree of indigestion is considerable, and the nutrition of the child is interfered with.

Colic is much more frequent in bottle-fed infants than in those fed on breast milk. Cow's milk, no matter how skillfully it is prepared for their use, is at best an unsuitable diet and taxes the digestive ability of robust children. It is quite natural for an infant whose digestive organs are not strong to develop colic and intestinal indigestion if put on artificial food. Any condition that causes indigestion may likewise cause colic. Those children who are always overfeeding,—taking too much milk, too strong milk, or who are fed irregularly,—are the colicky babies.

Constipation is frequently associated with colic and may be the actual cause. A daily movement of the bowel does not necessarily mean that the bowels are emptying themselves satisfactorily. Despite the daily movement, there may be considerable fecal matter left in the bowel which undergoes decomposition. This results in the evolution of large quantities of gas and severe attacks of colic. Indigestion is very often caused by conditions which effect the stability of the child's nervous organism; such conditions are fright, anger, fatigue, exhaustion, excitement.

The origin of the colic in breast-fed children is very [545] often caused by some nervous condition of the mother that affects her milk. Constipation in the mother may cause colic in the child.

Symptoms.—A baby having an attack of colic will cry loudly from time to time and whine during the interval; it will pull up its legs and bear down. Its abdomen is tense and hard and distended with gas. With the expulsion of the gas the pain ceases and the child falls asleep. If the attack is very severe the prostration and exhaustion is marked; the feet are cold and the body is bathed in perspiration.

If the colic is constant the child may be fretful and restless most of the time, being seemingly comfortable for only an hour or two in the twenty-four.

In older children who cry because of severe pain in the abdomen the possibility of appendicitis must not be forgotten.

Treatment.—Find out the cause of the colic if possible. If the cause is located in the mother, the remedy naturally must affect her. Regulation of her bowel, restriction of her diet, and proper exercise, may be sufficient to effect a cure of the colic in the infant.

The object of treatment is to help the child get rid of the gas. The best and quickest means to effect this is to apply massage or give a rectal injection. An injection of two ounces of cold water in which a half or one teaspoonful of glycerine has been put, will act quickly. Dry heat applied to the abdomen in the form of the hot-water bottle or woolen cloths will aid in the expulsion of the gas. The feet should be kept warm.

In cases of habitual colic in breast-fed babies the cause may be in the quality of the mother's milk. It should be examined and if found too strong should be diluted. This can be done by giving the child an ounce of plain boiled water or barley water before each feeding. If the child gets an ounce of liquid before each feeding he will not want as much of the breast milk; so we shall have the same total quantity, but a reduced quality, which may cure the colic at once.

It is necessary, in order to cure colic, that the bowels move every day in a satisfactory manner. If any aid [546] is needed, milk of magnesia is the best laxative. It may be given in teaspoonful doses in water previous to a feeding. Aromatic cascara sagrada in from ten to thirty-drop doses is a very good laxative, if a stronger remedy is needed.

To relieve the acute attack, three drops of Hoffman's anodyne may be given in two teaspoonfuls of warm water and repeated in ten-minute intervals until relieved, to a baby under one year of age. From five to ten drops of gin, given in three teaspoonfuls of warm water, and repeated in fifteen minutes, is also satisfactory and harmless. A very good remedy which may be used with the above for quick relief, and to stop the child from crying, is the following: Fold a piece of flannel cloth (two thicknesses) the size of the baby's abdomen; wring out of very hot water and drop ten drops of turpentine over the surface,—at different spots,—of the flannel and lay on abdomen,—turpentine side next skin. Cover this with another piece of flannel,—two or three thicknesses, that has been dry-heated and allow to remain in place for about ten minutes.

Colic, as a rule, disappears completely about the third month.

APPENDICITIS

Appendicitis is mentioned here merely to acquaint mothers with its prominent symptoms.

When a child has what seems to be an attack of indigestion, but complains of pain and tenderness in the abdomen, vomits, and develops a fever, and is constipated, appendicitis may be suspected.

The pain and tenderness are not referred to the region of the appendix but are more centrally located. If, however, the finger point is pressed over the appendix, distinct tenderness will be elicited in inflammation of that region. Constipation is the rule in appendicitis, but diarrhea occasionally accompanies it.

The abdominal muscles may be rigid, that is, the abdomen does not feel soft as is usual; there is a feeling if they are pressed, as if they were hard and unyielding.

Treatment.—Put the child in bed and send for the family physician at once. The condition is too serious [547] and too uncertain to delay, or for a parent to make any effort at treatment. Appendicitis is a much more serious condition in infancy and childhood than it is in an adult.

JAUNDICE IN INFANTS

There are two types of jaundice in infants that deserve brief consideration.

1st. There is a form of jaundice caused by a defect in the development of the bile or gall tubes. These infants develop jaundice a day or two after birth and become intensely jaundiced within a very brief time. They lose flesh and strength to a marked degree and die in a few weeks. It is not possible to affect this condition favorably by any method of treatment. This type of jaundice is not very common.

2nd. There is a type of jaundice that appears between the second and fifth day of life that is very common. It lasts from one to two weeks and then disappears. It is never fatal and is not serious. It requires no treatment.

JAUNDICE IN OLDER CHILDREN—CATARRHAL JAUNDICE—GASTRO DUODENITIS

Symptoms.—This form of jaundice begins like an attack of ordinary indigestion. There are, as a rule, pain, fever, vomiting, and prostration. The pain is located in the upper part of the abdomen and may be quite severe. The vomiting may continue for a number of days. The bowels are usually constipated. After a few days the jaundice sets in and may be quite intense. After the jaundice is established the stools are gray or white in color and there is much gas in the bowel. The urine is very dark and may be yellow or yellowish-green in color. The child complains of headache, is dull and listless, and appears sick and weak. The condition lasts about two weeks, but the jaundice may last much longer. It is not a serious disease.

Treatment.—The diet should be cut down in quantity and should consist of rare meat, fruit, and a small quantity of milk. If vomiting continues the milk may diluted with lime water or vichy water. The child [548] should drink water or vichy water freely. No starchy foods, or fats, or sugars should be allowed. The bowels should be kept open with calomel, one-tenth of a grain every hour until ten are taken, to be followed by citrate of magnesia every morning. If the pain is severe it may be relieved by a mustard paste or a turpentine poultice. The child should be given acid hydrochloric diluted, eight drops in one-half glass of water, ten minutes before each meal—and kept on it for at least one month.

INTESTINAL WORMS

There are three types of intestinal worms; they are known as the round-worm, the thread-worm, and the tape worm.

Round-Worm.—The round-worm is usually found in children of the run-about age. It is never seen in infancy. It occupies the small or upper intestine, and is from four to ten inches long. If there are round-worms in the bowel, there are usually a number of them and there may be hundreds.

Symptoms.—Round-worms give no definite symptoms. The only possible way to tell if they are present is actually to see them in the stools of the child. They are of a light gray color.

It is reasonable to expect that a child suffering from worms will have symptoms of abdominal distress from time to time; indigestion with colic and much gas may be present; children lose their appetites and are nervous and restless; sleep is disturbed; they may grind their teeth and talk in their sleep, and they may pick their noses unnecessarily during the day. These symptoms may, however, accompany other conditions when no worms are present in the bowel. My observation has been that in children in whom worms were present the nervous symptoms were distinctly accentuated. They are unreliable children; they seem well to-day and peevish to-morrow; they complain of headaches, dizziness, and chilly feelings. They are hysterical, noisy, uncontrollable. A child with these symptoms should be suspected of having worms and if no cause can be found to explain his temperamental vagaries he should [549] be treated for worms. I have cured a number of children of excessive nervousness by giving them medicine for worms when no worms were present. Such results can only be explained on the assumption that these children were suffering from intestinal auto-toxemia or self-poisoning, and the thorough disinfection of the bowel apparently stopped the process by ridding the child's system of a mass of bacteria, which were undoubtedly causing the auto-toxemia and consequent nervousness.

Treatment.—The most efficient remedy for removing round-worms is Santonin. The quantity necessary for the various ages is as follows:

Two to four years   2   grains.

Four to six years   3   grains.

Six to ten years   3-1/2 grains.

The best way to give it is in divided doses, with an equal quantity of sugar of milk. For a child of six years the formula would therefore be, 3-1/2 grains of Santonin, mixed with the same quantity of sugar of milk divided into three powders. These powders are given four hours apart in the following way. The child is given a light supper the evening before and one-half glass citrate of magnesia the following morning and the first powder one-half hour later; no breakfast being given. A light lunch, of milk and crackers, may be taken about noon. The second powder is given four hours after the first, and the third four hours after the second. Half an hour after the last powder, a dose of castor oil (one tablespoonful) is given. In a few moments the bowels will move; usually there are no worms in this movement. A little later they will move freely again and if worms are present they will be discharged in this movement.

Thread-Worm, or Pin-Worm.—A thread-worm looks just like a little piece of white thread. They are found in the lower part of the bowel and in the rectum. They are usually present, if present at all, in large numbers.

Symptoms.—The chief symptom is itching. It may be limited to the anus or it may involve the neighboring [550] parts. Thread-worms may find their way out of the anus and in female children may find their way into the vagina. In these instances the child is tormented with itching of the privates and may establish the habit of self-abuse as a result of the constant itching and scratching. The itching is more intense at night soon after the child goes to bed. As a result of the local irritation in the lower part of the bowel and rectum there is set up a catarrh of the bowel which produces large quantities of mucus.

Treatment.—The only medication by the mouth that is of any use is turpentine in one drop doses after meals, given in a teaspoonful of sugar. The best treatment, and in most cases the only treatment that is effective, is the use of rectal injections. The procedure is as follows:—The child first gets a cleaning injection of two quarts of warm water into which a teaspoonful of borax has been put. This will wash away any mucus or fecal matter that may have collected. This injection is best given with a No. 18 rectal catheter which is pushed into the rectum for about 10 inches, the water being allowed to run away as it enters. From six to eight ounces of the infusion of quassia is then passed, as high up as the catheter will reach. It is intended that the quassia will remain in as long as possible, for at least half an hour. In order to assure this there are two features that should be kept in mind: first, the water should be allowed to flow in slowly, consequently hold the bag low, not higher than two feet above the level of the bed on which the patient lies; second, after the water is all in remove the catheter very slowly and keep the child absolutely quiet. This treatment is repeated every second night for a week, then twice a week for four weeks.

A solution of garlic is a very effective remedy and may be tried if the quassia fails, which is not likely if the treatment is carried out effectively and if the parts are kept scrupulously clean.

Tape Worms.—Tape worms are obtained from eating raw meat, pork or sausage, rarely from fish, and from playing with cats and dogs. [551]

Symptoms.—No definite symptoms accompany the presence of tape worm. The children may have pains in the abdomen, diarrhea, a capricious appetite, foul breath, and they may suffer from anemia, sometimes quite severely. The only positive symptoms is the presence of links of the worm in the stools.

Treatment.—Give a dose of castor oil at bed time. Two hours after breakfast next morning give one-half dram of the oleoresin of male-fern in emulsion or capsule. Very light nourishment should be taken during the day, composed of gruels and soups. When the worm is passed it should be examined to find if the head is present; if not, the treatment should be repeated in twenty-four hours.

RUPTURE

Rupture of any description is not a condition that any mother should attempt to treat. A physician should be called in every case. Any misdirected effort at manipulation or pressure may result in irreparable injury to the parts. External applications are useless and may be injurious.

All ordinary forms of rupture in infancy and early childhood are curable if properly treated. [552]

[553]

CHAPTER XXXVI

DISEASES OF CHILDREN, CONTINUED

Mastitis or Inflammation of the Breasts in Infancy—Mastitis in Young Girls—Let Your Ears Alone— Never Box a Child's Ears—Do Not Pick the Ears—Earache—Inflammation of the Ear—Acute Otitis—Swollen Glands—Acute Adenitis—Swollen Glands in the Groin—Boils—Hives— Nettle Rash—Prickly Heat—Ringworm in the Scalp— Eczema—Poor Blood—Simple Anemia—Chlorosis—Severe Anemia—Pernicious Anemia

MASTITIS, OR INFLAMMATION OF THE BREASTS IN INFANCY

There are a few drops of a milky secretion in the breasts of infants when born. Occasionally the amount will be in excess of the normal quantity, and the breasts, around the nipple, may be swollen and slightly inflamed. Should this condition persist, it may be relieved by painting the parts with the tincture of belladonna. Under no circumstances should the breasts be manipulated or rubbed, as this is very apt to cause an inflammatory condition, and to result in mastitis.

Mastitis begins, as a rule, during the second week of life. The breast becomes red, swollen, painful, and shows inflammatory changes. It may terminate without the formation of an abscess, or it may go on to suppuration. The child becomes extremely restless and irritable, it is disinclined to nurse, and suffers from loss of sleep and nourishment. It is possible for such a condition, in the female, to injure the breast to the extent of arresting its development and to render it useless in the future. If the suppuration is extensive the process may terminate fatally.

Mastitis in infants is caused by unnecessary interference and manipulation and by want of cleanliness. When it occurs the parts should be kept absolutely clean and should not be handled in any way. Ichthyol 25 per [554] cent., Zinc Oxide Ointment, enough to make one ounce, spread upon old, clean, soft linen, and laid over the parts and changed every six hours, is an excellent healing application. A piece of oiled silk may be put outside the linen to prevent the ointment staining the clothing, and over this a layer of absorbent cotton and a binder, applied without pressure.

If an abscess develops in spite of treatment, it must be freely opened and freely drained, and the general health of the patient supported by regular nourishment and tonics.

Mastitis in Young Girls.—Pain and swelling of the breasts are sometimes complained of by girls between the twelfth and fifteenth years, though it may occur at an earlier or later date. If left alone the condition will invariably subside without treatment. Should bacteria find an entrance through the nipple at this time, an abscess may result. The whole breast is involved and it will be exceedingly painful and much swollen. There may be moderate fever, headache, and a pronounced feeling of indisposition. These patients should be given a laxative,—citrate of magnesia, or Pluto Water, and kept on a very light diet. An ice-bag should be kept constantly at the breast during the day, and a moist dressing of 1:5000 bichloride of mercury during the night.

It may take a week before recovery takes place.

LET YOUR EARS ALONE

Never Box a Child's Ears.—A single blow may make a child deaf; repeated blows on their ears will certainly injure children's hearing.

Thomas A. Edison, our greatest inventor, was made deaf when a lad by a surly brakeman, who soundly boxed his ears for some trivial or fancied offense.

Boxing a child's ears is but one of a great many things you should never do to the ears. In fact, there are far more things you should not do to safeguard the hearing, than there are things you can do to benefit your ears.

Do Not Pick the Ears.—Do not put cotton in the ears unless ordered to do so by a reputable physician. Do not [555] syringe the ears without the doctor's orders. Put no poultices in the ears. Do not put drops of any kind in the ears unless prescribed by a doctor. Above all, do not use the advertised ear cures, as most of them are harmful. Never blow into a child's ear, never douche the nose without the doctor's orders, as this may wash germs into the tubes leading to the ears and bring about a serious condition.

Riding in tunnels, especially in tunnels under water where the air pressure varies, has, through some recent investigation, been found to be injurious to the ears of a great many people.

Conductors and other trainmen who run through many tunnels are apt to have ear trouble, as are the men who work underground a great depth where they are in motion, such as miners running underground trains.

If you have an earache that continues for any length of time, take no chances, but consult a physician. And remember to care for the throat and nose, as ill conditions in those places result in ear troubles. Do not blow your nose too hard; it merely injures the inner sides of the ear drums. Adenoids in children frequently bring about a bad ear trouble. Even seasickness is due in a great measure to ear disturbances.

If you have a running ear, attend to it at once by visiting a doctor. So serious is this that life insurance companies will not insure people in that condition.

Earache.—When a child complains of earache its ear should be examined. In nearly every case of earache it is necessary to treat the throat, as this is, as a rule, the seat of the trouble. An antiseptic gargle of equal parts of Borolyptol and warm water is an excellent mixture. It should be used freely every two hours. Children suffering from earache should be kept indoors. If the examination should show that it is not necessary to lance the ear drum, some local measure may be adopted to allay the pain.

Putting the child in bed with the head resting on a hot-water bottle may be all that will be necessary. The following procedure may be carried out, but only after a physician has made an examination and according to his directions: A hot water douche, given by means of a [556] douche bag, is quite effective. The water should be 110° F.; the bag should be held about two feet above the level of the child's head, and the irrigating point should not be pushed into the ear, but held so that the water will find its own way into the ear.

When the earache does not respond to the above methods the ear should be closely watched and examined at intervals so that it may be opened at the right moment. This is very essential because, if it is neglected, the pus may find its way into the mastoid cells and set up the dangerous disease, mastoiditis. This disease may cause abscess of the brain and death. The moment a child develops fever in the course of an earache the ear should be examined and opened at once, if found necessary.

Inflammation of the Ear. Acute Otitis.—Inflammation of the ear seldom occurs in childhood, unless as a complication, or as a result of some infectious disease. Any disease which affects the throat in any way may be the cause of the inflammation of the ear. Such diseases are, "cold in the head," tonsilitis, grippe, "sore throat," or pharyngitis, measles, scarlet fever. It is much more common in children than in adults. The younger the child, the more liable it is to develop ear trouble when suffering from any of the above diseases. The presence of adenoids favors the development of ear complications.

Symptoms.—There is one symptom present in all cases of inflammation of the ear; that is, fever. Pain may or may not be present; it is present in a majority of the cases. Children with inflammation of the ear are exceedingly restless and do not sleep long at a time nor do they sleep soundly.

Treatment.—The treatment is to open the drum membrane, at the right time, which of course will always be done by a physician who has had some experience in this work.

After Treatment.—The after treatment consists of washing or syringing the ear every three hours with eight or twelve ounces of a 1:10,000 solution of corrosive sublimate. This will be kept up for four days; then the intervals between the washing will be extended to five hours, and kept up until the drum membrane closes. If [557] the corrosive sublimate solution should cause any eruption around the ear, a normal salt solution (see page 627) may be used in the same way, and in the same quantity as above. A running ear will run for from three to six weeks. It may heal up at any time after ten days. If the discharge should suddenly stop and the fever rise, it indicates that the opening has become plugged or healed too quickly. In either case it will have to be opened again. As soon as the ear begins running again the symptoms will disappear. After syringing the ear it should be dried thoroughly with pieces of sterile absorbent cotton.

The best syringe to use for washing out the ear is a one-ounce hard-rubber ear syringe with a soft rubber tip. An ordinary douche bag will do if a syringe of the above character cannot be obtained. The douche bag should not be held higher than two feet above the patient's head. The double-current ear irrigator is an excellent device for this purpose. The child should be on its back on a table. Its arms should be fastened down by its side. A basin can be placed under its ear and the irrigating done without causing any pain or discomfort.

Any child addicted to disease of the ear should be closely watched and examined for tuberculosis. Scrofula may accompany this condition. These children need careful attention in every little detail, they need good nourishment, fresh air night and day, and they should not be pushed at school. During the winter they should be protected from "catching colds;" it is a good plan to put them on a cod-liver-oil mixture for the entire cold season. During the summer they should have a radical change of climate.

SUMMARY:

1st. Inflammation of the ear is frequently a complication of or follows some other disease which affects the throat.

2nd. If a child with one of these diseases becomes restless, sleepless and feverish, be on the look-out for ear trouble. [558]

3rd. The ear must be lanced immediately when necessary.

4th. The after treatment is very important, because the hearing of the child depends upon it.

SWOLLEN GLANDS. ACUTE ADENITIS

Swollen glands in infancy and childhood are usually seen below and behind the ear, less frequently in the groin. Their cause is, as a rule, local disturbance in the mouth or throat, as decayed teeth, enlarged tonsils, cold in the head, catarrh, adenoids, or some form of infection of the mouth, or throat, or scalp. They occasionally accompany scarlet fever, diphtheria, measles, and influenza. They seldom suppurate.

Symptoms.—A swelling is noticed just below the angle of the jaw; it does not grow rapidly. There is a slight temperature and the child is more or less irritable. If the patient is an infant, the fever may be quite high and there may be considerable prostration. The trouble lasts from four to eight weeks.

Treatment.—An ice-bag constantly applied is the best treatment. This not only relieves pain, but it prevents the possibility of the gland breaking down and suppurating. It is sometimes difficult to keep an ice-bag on an infant, in which case cold compresses should be applied. These are made by taking several layers of old linen or cheese cloth and laying them on ice. They should be applied frequently to the swollen gland. The following ointment may be applied, though the ice-bag is the better and more certain treatment: Ichthyol 25 per cent., Adeps Lanae one ounce. This is applied on cloth and renewed every six hours.

This ointment is black and stains the clothing. For that reason it is advised to use oiled silk over the cloth to avoid staining the pillow or clothing.

Children suffering from adenitis should use a spray of Dobell's solution in the nose and throat three or four times daily. If the cause of the swollen glands is known, treatment for its cure should be promptly instituted.

In the event of pus forming the gland must be opened and drained. [559]

Swollen glands in the groin of a child are caused most frequently by some inflammatory condition of the privates, which should be discovered and treated.

BOILS

In some delicate children and in some children who do not seem to be delicate, repeated crops of boils may appear from time to time.

It is necessary to open them as soon as pus is present. They should be pressed out and a gauze dressing, wet with a saturated solution of boric acid, bound over them. The dressing should be kept moist.

I have in a number of instances successfully rid a child of the tendency to boils by the use of the following formula, which I can recommend highly as one of the best tonics I have ever used in the treatment of delicate and poorly nourished children: Tinct. Nux Vomica 4 drops, Acid Phosphoric Dilute 8 drops, Syrup Hypophosphites, 1 teaspoonful. Make a two-ounce mixture and give to children over four years of age one teaspoonful after each meal; to younger children, one-half teaspoonful after each meal.

It is necessary in these cases to keep the bowels open daily.

HIVES. NETTLE-RASH

Cause.—Contact with different plants, bites of insects, irritation from clothing, use of certain drugs. Certain articles of food, such as tomatoes, strawberries, oatmeal, buckwheat, have all been said to cause hives.

Dentition during warm weather and the presence of worms and chronic malarial poisoning have been known to cause hives.

It is most frequently caused, however, in childhood by some disturbance in the stomach or bowels.

It causes severe itching and loss of sleep and as a result of these the general health suffers.

Treatment.—If caused by any external irritant, remove it. If it is caused by any special article of diet, prohibit its use. If no cause is apparent, give the child one tablespoonful of castor oil, and put it on the mildest diet possible of soups, broths, and dried stale bread. Give no [560] milk. Use the following treatment on the erupted parts: Menthol, ten grains in one ounce of cold cream. Keep the bowels open.

It is sometimes necessary to advise a change of air before complete cure results.

PRICKLY HEAT

This is a very common complaint in children during the summer months. It is so common that it is well known and easily recognized. It consists of a bright red eruption, composed of little papules, close together.

The rash comes out quickly, so much so that mothers may be surprised and frightened by observing an angry looking rash on their baby some morning when none was there the night before. It most frequently appears upon the neck, back, chest, and forehead. It is exceedingly itchy and a child may scratch itself and cause extensive harm. Eczema, of a very obstinate type, frequently results from scratching.

The rash of prickly heat is easily diagnosed from other rashes because it is accompanied by no other symptom, such as fever, which would suggest a more serious disease. The rash of prickly heat resembles the rash of scarlet fever more than any other rash, but it is quickly noted that when a child has scarlet fever it has every symptom of being profoundly sick, while prickly heat has no symptom other than the itch and discomfort. It is caused by overfeeding, being overclothed, and sweating in hot weather.

Treatment.—Steps should be taken to prevent prickly heat in an infant. Use light, seasonable clothing, bathe frequently, and use plenty of good toilet powder. When the child actually has an attack, open its bowels freely with citrate of magnesia, and give some sweet spirits of niter, according to age. Protect the skin from the irritating underwear by interposing a soft piece of linen. In order to reduce the inflammation and cure the condition apply equal parts of starch and boric acid powder freely. Keep the patient on a light fluid diet. The bran bath is advisable if the little patient is addicted to these skin eruptions. [561]

RINGWORM OF THE SCALP

Children of all ages are liable to "catch" ringworm of the scalp. It particularly affects those who are untidy, dirty, and badly cared for, though any child is apt to get it while attending the public schools.

If a mother discovers scaly patches in the scalp, with loss of hair, ringworm should be immediately suspected. It is not, however, always easy to diagnose the condition, especially if the case is a mild one. If it is a severe attack, there is, as a rule, quite a little inflammation, and this may render the condition obscure for some time. The disease may be mistaken for dandruff, but dandruff covers a large area of the scalp, while ringworm is limited and sharply defined. Dandruff may cause a loss of hair; if it does, the hairs come out clean, while in ringworm they break off near the scalp.

Treatment.—Ringworm is always curable, provided the patient is watched and treatment carried out thoroughly. It is always absolutely necessary to treat the condition, because it will not get better of itself, and the longer it is permitted to last, the worse it gets, and the more difficult it is to cure. If treatment is begun at once, it may take two months to cure it. If the case has lasted for some time, or if it has been neglected and not treated thoroughly, it will take from six months to one year to cure it. These facts are stated so that parents may not become discouraged.

The first thing to do is to cut the hair as close to the scalp as possible, wherever the ringworm is, and for about an inch outside, and all around it. The entire scalp should be thoroughly washed three times a week. The scales should be kept soft by the use of carbolic soap.

The hair should not be brushed at all, because brushing the hair may spread the disease to other parts of the scalp. Every child with ringworm of the scalp should wear a cap of muslin or one lined with paper, so that others may not be infected. These caps can be burned when dirty and new ones made. One of the best remedies to apply to the affected area is the following: Bichloride [562] of mercury, 2 grains; olive oil, 2 teaspoonfuls; kerosene, 2 teaspoonfuls. This is rubbed in every day until the parts are sore and tender. It is a good plan to apply this mixture to the entire scalp every fourth day, to guard against other parts becoming infected. It is not necessary to rub it in when using it where there is no ringworm.

When the scalp becomes sore from the application it can be stopped for a day or two, or until better; then begin again and repeat the treatment right along. If the kerosene in the above mixture is objected to, a very good mixture is bichloride of mercury, 2 grains, and tincture of iodine, 1 ounce. This may be rubbed vigorously enough to produce a rash. If the disease shows a tendency to spread under this treatment it is best to apply the latter mixture to the entire scalp.

Ringworm on any other part of the body is effectually treated by applying tincture of iodine. It should be painted on every day until the skin begins to peel, when the ringworm will disappear with the skin.

ECZEMA

Eczema is the most important skin disease of babyhood. It is probably the most frequent skin disease of infancy. Any baby may develop eczema. There are, however, some babies who seem to be very susceptible to it. The reason of this susceptibility seems to be due to the natural tenderness, or delicacy, of the skin. These children, because of the extreme sensitiveness of the skin, develop an eczema from a very slight degree of external irritation, or a trifling disturbance of digestion. Children of rheumatic or gouty parents are more liable to be victims of eczema than are others. Eczema of the face is quite common in children who are apparently healthy and fat. It does not seem to matter whether they are breast-fed or bottle-fed. The following conditions may be regarded as contributory to eczema:

Exposure to winds; cold, dry air; heat; the use of hard water or strong soaps; lack of cleanliness, and the irritation of clothing. It frequently accompanies chronic constipation, indigestion, and other conditions of the [563] intestinal canal; overfeeding; too early or too excessive use of starchy foods.

Eczema of the Face:—Eczema Rubrum.—This is the most frequent form. It affects the cheeks, scalp, forehead, and sometimes the ears and the neck. It begins on the cheeks as small red papules. These join together and form a mass of moist, exuding crusts. They dry in time and may be so thick as to form a mask on the face. The skin may be much swollen. When the crusts are removed the face looks red and angry and bleeds easily. It is exceedingly itchy. It causes restlessness, loss of sleep, and it may affect the appetite, though, as a rule, the health remains good. Eczema of the face is exceedingly chronic; it improves from time to time, but it is cured with great difficulty only.

Infants suffering with eczema of the face begin to improve about the middle of the second year and may be entirely cured about this time. The reason of this is the greater amount of exercise the child is getting at this period. If the disease continues longer it is because of the unnecessary amount of fat that the child has.

Treatment.—Eczema is a notoriously tedious disease. There is very little tendency for it to improve, if left to itself. The age, the severity, and just how much you can rely upon the mother, or nurse, faithfully to carry out directions—upon these its cure depends. At best, the treatment may have to be carried out for months. If the eczema is accompanied with constipation and indigestion in infancy, very little can be done with the eczema until these conditions are removed.

There exists in the minds of the laity, and in some physicians also, an idea that it is wrong, or dangerous, to cure, or "dry up," an eczema. It is never dangerous, but highly desirable, to cure an eczema, whenever possible. It is always wise, because it is always necessary, to get the child in perfect condition before you treat the eczema. Cure the constipation, or indigestion, or cold, or whatever is the matter with the child; then treat the eczema. This is the only plan that offers any success. It is not a simple matter to find out why a nursing child [564] is having indigestion. The most minute care must be exercised to find out the element in the milk that is causing the eczema. It would, however, be foolish, and a waste of time, to apply pastes, etc., to an eczema of the face, while the real cause that produced it was still in existence. It will frequently be found necessary to change the food entirely. Strict attention to the bowels is essential, both in infants and in older children. Sometimes to cure the constipation means an immediate cure of the eczema.

If the child is anemic, poorly nourished, and flabby, tonics are advisable. Cod liver oil is of use in quite a number of these cases. Eczematous children should not be taken out when the weather is very cold or when there are high winds. They should not be washed with plain water, or with castile soap and water. When washing is necessary, do it with milk and water, to which one teaspoonful of borax is added. The clothing must not be too heavy.

In eczema of the face, the child must either wear a mask or heavy woolen gloves, so that he will not scratch the parts. Frequently these fail, and it will be necessary to restrain the child from scratching the face by the use of some mechanical device. A piece of strong pasteboard bandaged on the elbows, so as to prevent the child from bending them, is all that is necessary. If the child cannot bend the elbows he cannot scratch his face, yet he has the free use of his hands.

The use of external remedies is imperative, as frequently the cause is mostly external, and in other cases it must be used in addition to the general treatment. Before external treatment is instituted, the crusts should be softened by applying olive oil to them for twenty-four hours, after which they can be removed with soap and water. If there is much inflammation, or if the face looks angry, a very good application is Lassar's paste.

Later, when the inflammation has subsided and the itching is severe, a mixture of tar ointment, 3 teaspoonfuls; zinc oxide, 1-1/2 teaspoonfuls; rose water ointment, 6 teaspoonfuls has proved to be one of the very best.

When the eczema on the face is of the weeping, or [565] moist, variety, the application of bassorin paste gives splendid results.

When an external remedy is applied to any eczematous surface it is necessary to apply it on a cloth. Simply to smear it on will do no good.

In the treatment of eczema, when the children are breast-fed, it is well to remember that the real cause of the eczema may be in the mother. If the mother is constipated, or if her diet is too liberal, if she is drinking beer, or an excess of coffee, or is not taking exercise, the eczema may be caused by one or other or all of these.

For eczema of the scalp the remedy to use is white-precipitate ointment, 1 part; vaseline, 4 parts. Mix together and apply.

POOR BLOOD. SIMPLE ANEMIA

Causes.—There is what may be termed an unnatural tendency toward poor blood during infancy and childhood. The explanation of this anomalous condition is, that the tax or strain put upon the blood to provide for the growth of the child is severe, and is in addition to the great demands made upon it in the exercise of its regular duties. We must, therefore, always take this special duty into consideration, when the question of recuperation, convalescence, feeding, and the administration of blood foods and tonics comes up.

It is not necessary to specify the diseases from which a child may suffer and recover, in an anemic condition. Any disease may leave a child with temporarily poor blood. The conditions which most frequently produce anemia in childhood are improper feeding and unhealthy surroundings. It is not fully appreciated how seriously these conditions can affect the health of growing children. There is one condition that every mother should be warned against, namely, the possibility of unduly prolonging breast-feeding. Children should be weaned at the end of the tenth month. By prolonging the breast-feeding a mother can undermine the vitality and strength of her baby and so impoverish its blood as to invite disease. A bottle-fed baby should be put upon a mixed diet at the same time. To continue feeding a child exclusively on [566] milk for a year or two after weaning, simply because "it will not take anything else," is criminal. Any woman guilty of such stupidity should never have become a mother. Once again it must be emphasized that every child must have an abundance of fresh air, must not be confined in close, hot, unsanitary rooms, and must have a daily, satisfactory movement of the bowels to be a healthy child with good blood in its body.

Symptoms.—Children suffering from poor blood are flabby, constipated, hungry, weak specimens of childhood. They are under weight, complain of headache, pains, disturbed sleep, are nervous and irritable. They tire quickly, are short of breath, and may have a tendency to faint easily. The hands and feet are cold, the pulse is small and irregular. They may have attacks of nose-bleeding and of bed-wetting.

Chlorosis.—Chlorosis is that form of anemia, of poor blood, which occurs in young girls about the time their sickness begins. It is most frequently seen between the fourteenth and seventeenth years, and more often in blondes than in brunettes. The cause is not known. It is thought to be due to constipation. Any occupation which is deleterious to health has a distinct influence on the condition. Employment in factories, confinement in badly ventilated rooms, bad or insufficient food, great grief, care, or a bad fright, mental strain, overstudy, may all produce, or contribute to the production of chlorosis.

Symptoms.—The symptoms of chlorosis resemble those of simple anemia. Children suffering from anemia are pale; girls with chlorosis have a peculiar greenish yellow tint in the skin. They are short of breath, they have vertigo, palpitation, disturbances of digestion, constipation, cold hands and feet, and scanty or arrested monthly periods. They have various nervous disturbances, such as headache, pains in various parts of the body, neuralgia, especially over the eyes, hysterical attacks, and sometimes cholera. Ulcer of the stomach is sometimes seen in this condition.

The disease lasts for a year or longer; it frequently lasts a number of years. Relapses are frequent.

By permission of Henry H. Goddard
"A Misfortune at Birth"

Warren is feeble-minded. His family said it was due to "a serious fall of the mother."

[A] "The family history is, however, exceedingly interesting.

"The paternal grandfather, whom we have called Nick, was of good family, although he himself was totally different from the rest. He was weak in every way, and to be considered feeble-minded. He married into a family that was much lower socially than his own, although we have no proof that it was a defective family. The children of this couple were all mentally defective and low-grade, morally as well as intellectually.

"Warren's father, Jake, a thoroughly disgraceful character, married Sal, a woman somewhat older than he.

"The immorality of this family beggars description. A girl named Moll was fifteen years old when Jake brought her into his home: his wife, Sal, was so feeble-minded that she allowed the illicit relations between these two. Moll's child was born in the hospital after the mother had been sent away from one Home because of her horrible syphilitic condition—from which she finally died.

"Our boy Warren's sister Liz with whom the father lived in incestuous relations, was also allowed to live illicitly with a man who worked for her father. She was so simple that she talked openly about her relations with her father and with this man. When a child was to be born the man married her.

"This is not all, but enough: and sufficient to show what feeble-mindedness leads to when it takes the direction of sexual abuses."

[A],"Feeble-mindedness: Its Causes and Consequences," Goddard, The Macmillan Company.

[567] **Severe Anemia: Pernicious Anemia.**—This is the most severe form of anemia, or the condition in which we have the poorest blood. While this condition frequently results in death the others rarely ever do. This condition is not common in childhood.

Symptoms.—There is intense weakness and prostration. The skin is very pale, the mucous membranes are bluish white. The breath is markedly short and there is often dropsy of the limbs and feet. Fever is often present and quite high. The disease lasts a number of months; the patient often feels better for a time, then relapses into a more serious condition than before.

TREATMENT OF THE VARIOUS FORMS OF ANEMIA

Simple Anemia.—Find the cause and stop it. In infancy special attention should be given to diet and hygiene, giving the child plenty of fresh air, and a change of air to the country or seashore if necessary. The general treatment is more important than any benefit that may be derived from drugs. The rules laid down in the articles on "Malnutrition" must be closely followed in these children.

Chlorosis.—In this form of anemia, or poor blood, it is best to give iron. Change of air and change of scene are of special importance in these cases and will frequently cure. The general condition of course must not be overlooked. The diet, exercise, bowels, habits, should receive careful attention. Iron should be continued for a number of months after all traces of the anemia have disappeared.

Pernicious Anemia.—For this condition arsenic is the one remedy needful. In all conditions of poor blood the most careful attention should be given to the general health. Colds must be guarded against. The patients should never get their feet or their clothes wet. Muscular exercise, because of the weak condition of the heart, should be moderate, and only given on the advice of a physician. It is frequently necessary to stop all forms of exercise and in many instances we get the best results by directing complete rest in bed for a considerable part of the day or for all day if the case demands it. [568]

[569]

CHAPTER XXXVII

DISEASES OF CHILDREN, CONTINUED

Rheumatism—Malaria—Rashes of Childhood—Pimples—Acne—Blackheads— Convulsions—Fits—Spasms—Bed-wetting—Enuresis— Incontinence—Sleeplessness—Disturbed Sleep—Nightmare— Night Terrors—Headache—Thumb-sucking—Biting the Finger Nails—Colon Irrigation—How to Wash Out the Bowels —A High Enema—Enema—Methods of Reducing Fever —Ice Cap—Cold Sponging—Cold Pack—The Cold Bath—Various Baths—Mustard Baths—Hot Pack —Hot Bath—Hot Air, or Vapor Bath—Bran Bath —Tepid Bath—Cold Sponge—Shower Bath—Poultices —Hot Fomentations—How to Make and How to Apply a Mustard Paste—How to Prepare and Use the Mustard Pack—Turpentine Stupes—Oiled Silk, What it is and Why it is Used.

RHEUMATISM

This is a rather common disease of childhood. It occurs most frequently between the ages of nine and thirteen years. Children can have it, however, at any age.

The symptoms of rheumatism in children are much the same, though somewhat milder, as when the disease is present in an adult. Children are not quite as sick, nor is the fever as high, nor is the pain as great as in a grown person. In children the disease does not last as long, as a rule. Sometimes it will jump from one joint to another, and may, as a consequence, become chronic. When a child has once had rheumatism, it has the same disposition to recur that it has in adults. The principal danger of rheumatism in children is its tendency to attack the heart. Even mild attacks of the disease can do serious damage to the heart.

Children who have the rheumatic tendency invariably suffer from inflammatory conditions of the upper respiratory tract. They are prone to have recurring colds, tonsilitis, and sore throats. Treatment of conditions without regard to the underlying [570] rheumatism is never satisfactory. These children complain of indefinite pains, now in one place, now in another. These pains are commonly known as "growing-pains" and, inasmuch as they are rheumatic and not "growing pains," they should be regarded seriously because of the heart damage they might do if ignored, and especially so since the mildest attacks of rheumatism, without any joint symptoms even, frequently leave the heart in very bad shape. As a general rule it will be found that when a child has had a number of attacks of bronchitis or asthma it is rheumatic and should receive treatment for the rheumatic tendency.

Children with the tendency to rheumatism invariably eat too much red meats and sugar,—the latter in the form of candy or as an excess in the food.

Treatment of an Acute Attack.—The child should be put in bed and kept warm. The bowels should be freely opened with citrate of magnesia. The diet should be very light: milk and lime water or milk and vichy water, with a piece of dry toast or zwieback, is all the child needs until the fever is relieved. When a single joint is affected local measures may be taken for its relief. Wraping the joints up with flannel cloths which have been wrung out of true oil of wintergreen, and outside of this oiled silk snugly bandaged on, is an excellent external application. The flannel cloths should be kept moist by adding a little of the wintergreen from time to time as it dries in. This can be done without removing the bandage. This application is kept in place for twenty-four hours and renewed if necessary. Such an external application will aid in the actual cure of the disease and will quickly relieve the patient of the pain. The oil of wintergreen used in this way should be the "true" oil, and should be so specified when bought in the drug store.

Because of the great tendency to attack the heart a physician should take charge of every case of acute rheumatism in a child.

To Treat the Tendency to Rheumatism.—Exclude red meats and sugar in all forms as much as is possible. Give green vegetables freely, potatoes boiled with the skins on, fish, eggs, and poultry. Cereals with milk, [571] especially well cooked Scotch oatmeal, are exceedingly good for these children. By keeping up this diet after the acute attack has passed for a considerable time, it is possible to cure the various other complaints with which the child is afflicted,—tonsilitis, sore-throats, winter coughs, head-colds, bronchitis, asthma, etc.

These children should wear woolen underwear all the year round. They should be encouraged to drink water or vichy freely between meals.

In the treatment of an acute attack as given above it will be observed that no drugs are mentioned. This is intentional because it would be unjust to encourage the home treatment of a disease that is so treacherous, even in its mildest forms. Because of its tendency to recur and with each recurrence the danger of the heart being affected, it is advisable to put these children on cod liver oil or iron or some other good tonic. Every precaution should be taken to prevent these children from getting their feet wet or being out in the rain.

SUMMARY:—

Rheumatism is a dangerous disease in children.

In its mildest forms it can affect the heart badly.

It has a distinct tendency to recur.

Rheumatic children are afflicted with a number of diseased conditions which do not respond to treatment unless the rheumatism is treated.

Acute rheumatism should never be treated except by a physician because of its treacherous character.

MALARIA. INTERMITTENT FEVER

Malaria occurs quite often in infants and children. As a rule the child gives evidence of gastro-intestinal disturbance for a short period before the malarial symptoms appear. The chilly stage is often absent. Sometimes the hands and feet are cold and may be slightly blue and the child may appear to be in collapse. This stage may last for an hour or longer. The chilly stage may, however, be replaced by nervous symptoms,—restlessness, dizziness, [572] irritability, nausea, etc.,—or a convulsion may take place. In the second stage the temperature may rise quite high, the pulse may be quite rapid; the child is flushed, restless, and cries. This period may last from half an hour to two hours. The sweating stage is not as a rule well marked in a child. It may be very slight or not at all.

Between the attacks some children may be entirely well; others remain restless, have little appetite and poor digestion. Malaria in children does not always follow a typical course. We often see children suffering from spasms, fainting spells, neuralgias, diarrhea, vomiting, and skin eruptions, all due to the malarial condition. This often leads to a mistake in diagnosis. Intermittent fever is often mistaken for pneumonia. Malaria is not a favorable disease for an infant to have. It rapidly weakens the child and great debility and anemia follows.

Treatment.—The treatment for malaria in children is by the administration of quinine as in adults. It must, however, be given with care and intelligence; for this reason no mother should begin dosing her child with it without consulting a physician.

REGARDING MOSQUITOES

The following is an extract from a circular in relation to the causation and prevention of malaria and the life history and extermination of mosquitoes issued by the Department of Health, City of New York:

Extermination and Prevention of Mosquitoes.—Mosquitoes require for their development standing water. They cannot arise in any other way. A single crop soon dies and disappears unless the females find water on which their eggs may be laid. In order to prevent mosquitoes, therefore, the requirement is simple.

No Standing Water.—Pools of rain water, duck ponds, ice ponds, and temporary accumulations due to building; marshes, both of salt and fresh water, and road-side drains; pots, kettles, tubs, springs, barrels of water, and other back-yard collections, should be drained, filled with earth, or emptied.

Running streams should have their margins carefully cleaned and covered with gravel to prevent weeds and grass at the water's edge.

Lily ponds and fountain pools should, if possible, be abolished; if not, the margins should be cemented or carefully graveled, a good stock of minnows put in the water, and green slime (Algæ) regularly cleaned out, as it collects. [573]

Where tanks, cisterns, wells or springs are necessary to supply water, the openings to them should be closely covered with wire gauze (galvanized to prevent rusting), not the smallest aperture being left.

When neither drainage nor covering is practicable, the surface of the standing water should be covered with a film of light fuel oil (or kerosene) which chokes and kills the larvæ. The oil may be poured on from a can or from a sprinkler. It will spread itself. One ounce of oil is sufficient to cover 15 square feet of water. The oil should be renewed once a week during warm weather.

Particular attention should be paid to cess-pools. These pools when uncovered breed mosquitoes in vast numbers; if not tightly closed by a cemented top or by wire-gauze, they should be treated once a week with an excess of kerosene or light fuel oil.

Certain simple precautions suffice to protect persons living in malarial districts from infection:

First: Proper screening of the house to prevent the entrance of the mosquitoes (after careful search for and destruction of all those already present in the house), and screening of the bed at night. The chief danger of infection is at night (the Anopheles bite mostly at this time).

Second: The screening of persons in malarial districts who are suffering from malarial fever, so that mosquitoes may not bite them and thus become infected.

Third: The administration of quinine in full doses to malarial patients to destroy the malarial organisms in the blood.

Fourth: The destruction of mosquitoes by one or more of the methods already described.

These measures, if properly carried out, will greatly restrict the prevalence of the disease, and will prevent the occurrence of new malarial infections.

It must be remembered that when a person is once infected, the organisms may remain in the body for many years, producing from time to time relapses of the fever.

A case of malarial infection in a house (whether the person is actively ill or the infection is latent) in a locality where Anophele mosquitoes are present, is a constant source of danger, not only to the inmates of the house, but to the immediate neighborhood, if proper precautions are not taken. It should be noted in this connection that the mosquitoes may remain in a house through an entire winter and probably infect the inmates in the spring upon the return of the warm weather.

Malarial fever is prevalent in certain boroughs of New York City, and in view of the presence of standing water resulting from the extensive excavations taking place in various parts of these boroughs, is likely to extend, if means are not taken for its prevention.

REGULATIONS OF THE BOARD OF HEALTH, NEW YORK CITY, IN AID OF MOSQUITO EXTERMINATION AND THE PREVENTION OF MALARIAL FEVER

(In Force from March 15 to October 15.)

1. No rain-water barrel, cistern, or other receptacle for rain-water, shall be maintained without being tightly screened by netting, or so absolutely covered that no mosquito can enter.

2. No cans, pails, or anything capable of holding water, shall be thrown out or allowed to remain unburied on or about any premises.

3. Every uncovered cesspool or tank shall be kept in such condition that oil may be freely distributed so as to flow over the surface of the water. Covered cess-pools must have perfectly tight covers, and all openings must be screened.

4. No waste or other water shall be thrown out or allowed to stand on or near premises.

Information is requested as to the presence of standing water anywhere, so that the premises may be inspected and the legal remedies against the same be applied.

The prompt coöperation of all persons in the enforcement of the above regulations is earnestly desired, and they are assured that in this way the breeding of mosquitoes on their premises may be prevented.

Mosquitoes are, so far as known, the only means of conveying malaria.

"RASHES" OF CHILDHOOD

The following table gives all the characteristics of the rashes that accompany the eruptive fevers. The term "incubation" means the period of time which elapses between the time when the child was exposed to, or caught the disease, and the time when the child is taken sick. It is sometimes interesting to know where a child could have caught a disease; so if we know the incubation period we can tell exactly where the child was on the day, or days, when it was infected. [575]

Name	Incubation	Day of Rash	Character of Rash	Rash fades	Duration
Measles	10-14 days	4th day	Small red like spots resembling flea bites, first appearing on face and forehead, forming blotches with semi-lunar borders.	On the 7th day of fever	6-10 days
Scarlet	1-6 days occasionally longer	2d day of fever	Bright scarlet, rapidly diffused, first on chest and upper extremities	On 5th day of fever	8-9 days
Chicken-pox	4-12 days	2d day	Small rose vesicles, which do not become pustular	Slight scab of short duration	6-7 days
Typhoid Fever	10-14 days	7-14 days	Rose colored papules elevated, few in number, limited to trunk, disappear		From 21-35 days

Smallpox (Variola)	10-14 days	3d day of fever	Small, round, red hard, papules forming vescicles then pustules, first appearing on face and wrists on pressure	9th day scabs form and about 14th day fall off	14-21 days

Other Rashes.—There are so-called "stomach" rashes which are a source of much worry to mothers. These rashes may appear at any time and they may be limited to certain parts or may cover most of the body. They may be bright red, or they may be simply a general discoloration. They may appear as blotches or they may spread all over, like the rash of scarlet fever when at its height.

These rashes are of no importance, except that they indicate some derangement of the gastro-intestinal tract. As a rule they indicate indiscriminate feeding or overfeeding. Children who have had too much candy or pastries, or who have been fed things which are unsuited to their age, frequently develop rashes. Such children should have a thorough cleaning out; a dose of castor oil is probably the best cathartic to give them.

The mother may readily learn to know the difference between a rash that is unimportant and one that indicates one of the eruptive diseases, if she gives the matter a little careful thought. In the first place a child who is about to become the victim of one of the eruptive diseases will be sick, and will have a fever for two or three days before any rash appears; while on the other [576] hand a child may go to bed in good health and may next morning be covered with a general rash, or with large blotches, without any fever and without any evidence of ill-health, except the skin condition. In the second place, if the mother gives the child a cathartic and restricts the diet for a day the rash will disappear, and good spirits and good health will be maintained;

on the other hand, the giving of a cathartic to a child who is the victim of an eruptive disease will not tend to diminish the rash, but may accentuate it.

Pimples: Blackheads (Acne).—This eruption is situated chiefly on the face. It may appear, however, on the back, shoulders, and on the chest. It is mostly seen in young men and women about the age of puberty. It appears as conical elevations of the size of a pea; they are red and tender on pressure, and have a tendency to form matter, or pus, in their center. In from four to ten days the matter is discharged but the red spots continue for some time longer.

"Blackheads" appear as slightly elevated spots of a black color out of which a small worm-like substance may be pressed. Pimples and blackheads are due to inflammation of the glands of the skin. The mouths of these glands become filled with dust which acts as a plug causing the retention of the oily matter of the gland which becomes inflamed and hence the pimples and blackheads. Certain constitutional conditions favor the development of these skin blemishes. Constipation, indigestion, bad blood from unsanitary and bad hygienic surroundings, self-abuse and bad sexual habits favor the appearance of these skin affections.

Treatment.—The patient must avoid tea, coffee, tobacco, alcohol, veal, pork, fats, candy, pastries, cheese, and all edibles that are known to disagree with the digestion of the patient. Constipation must be avoided; if necessary, laxatives may be taken to keep the bowel open. The blackheads must be squeezed out with an instrument made for the purpose, not with the finger nails. Pimples must be opened with a sterile needle. The parts should be washed three times a day with hot water and green soap, and the following mixture applied at night:— [577]

Zinc Oxide   ounces 1/4

Powdered calamine   ounces 1/4

Lime water   ounce   6

Mix and shake before applying to the skin.

CONVULSIONS. FITS. SPASMS

Convulsions are quite common in children, especially those under three years of age.

A convulsion in an infant immediately, or within three months, after its birth is the result of injury, either at birth or later (a fall for example) which seriously affects the brain itself. After the third month the cause of fits or convulsions is, in a very large percentage of the cases, to be found in errors of diet resulting in disturbances in the stomach or bowels—eating of articles of food difficult to digest, as green or overripe fruit, salads, fresh bread, pickles, cheese, etc. Children of a nervous temperament are more liable to convulsions than are others. Females are more frequently victims of fits than are male children.

In infants convulsions often result from changes in the mother's milk. Mental excitement, deep emotion, anger, frights, severe affliction and distress will so affect a woman's milk that it will cause convulsions in her child if she nurses it while under the influence of any of these conditions.

Convulsions may result from any condition that disturbs the nutrition of the child, as, for example,—exhaustion, anemia, intestinal indigestion, blood poison, and general weakness resulting from some severe sickness, especially those of the digestive organs.

Various forms of brain disease cause spasms and fits; the most common are meningitis, tumors, hemorrhage, abscesses and injuries. Convulsions may accompany certain conditions, as, the presence of worms, teething, severe burns, foreign bodies in the ear, whooping cough, pneumonia scarlet fever, malaria, sometimes measles, typhoid fever, and diphtheria. Children who are badly nourished and who live constantly in unsanitary surroundings are more apt to have convulsions than those [578] who are well nourished and who live hygienically. One attack renders the patient more liable to another, and when the "habit" is established any trivial cause may incite a convulsion; persistent and systematic efforts should therefore be taken to prevent the attacks. The best preventives are:

1st. To regulate the diet and the bowels.

2nd. Remove adenoids and worms, if they exist.

3rd. Avoid the use of alcohol, coffee, tea, fresh bread, pastries, candies and all improper foods.

4th. Guard the child against catching cold, infectious diseases and all fevers. In other words, save the child from the cause and the convulsion will not take place.

By regulating the bowels we mean that everything the child eats must be seen by the mother, must be with the mother's permission, and must be suited to the child's age. If there is any question about the latter it will be advisable to have a physician write out a list of articles suitable to the child. It is generally necessary to eliminate meats, pastries, candies, sugar to a large extent, gravies, salads, sauces, and all the extras of the table, as pickles, mustard, relish, etc., as well as coffee, tea, cocoa, and alcohol.

The child should live in the open air as much as possible; a daily warm bath, followed by a quick, cold sponge, is a necessity.

Children subject to fits are possessed of a highly nervous temperament. They are difficult to manage unless managed with firmness and tact. It is not necessary to be harsh, but it is imperative to be firm and decided. They must be made to realize that they are not "the master," that their will is not supreme, and the mother must exact this condition; otherwise these children will become dictators and selfish despots—ruining the discipline of the home, spoiling their own chance of physical health, and rendering unhappy everyone around them. The parents, therefore, have a definite duty to perform and it is not an easy one. The food should be so regulated that each day a natural movement of the bowels will take place. (See article on constipation, page 303.) If a day should pass without a movement the child should be given a hot rectal enema as described on page586. [579]

The adenoids can be easily demonstrated to either exist or be absent. (See page 519.) If worms are known to be present in the child they should be at once removed. If they are simply suspected, the child should receive treatment for them, just the same. (See page 549.)

By going a long time without a convulsion the nervous system will recuperate itself, and become so strong and healthy that what once would cause a fit will make no impression in its new strengthened state; therefore, if you "save the child from the cause," the convulsions will cure themselves, as it were.

There are some cases of convulsions for which no satisfactory explanation can be found.

Treatment.—When a child has a convulsion, remove its clothing and put it into a mustard bath. The temperature of the bath should be 105° F. Every part of the child should be under the water except the head, which is supported in the palm of the hand. While it is in the bath its body, and especially its arms and legs, should be briskly rubbed by the hands of an assistant in order to keep the circulation active. A rectal injection of soap suds or plain salt and water (see page 579) should be given while the child is in the bath, because, as explained above, a large percentage of these cases are caused by gastro-intestinal derangements. The rectal injection will likely remove the cause. An ordinary convulsion lasts from five to ten minutes. When the child is removed from the bath it should be placed in a warm, comfortable bed and kept absolutely quiet. A hot-water bottle may be put near its feet and an ice-bag or cold cloths should be kept on its head. It should be given a full dose of castor oil and allowed to go to sleep. Its diet should consist of light broths for two or three days and during this time it should not be disturbed or annoyed by too much attention. This is as far as it is wise or safe for any mother to go in the treatment of convulsions. A physician should be called in every instance, because a convulsion should never be regarded lightly. Many children have become idiots, others have been afflicted with paralysis, because of inattention at the proper time. [580]

SUMMARY:—

1st. Convulsions must always be regarded as serious.

2nd. Convulsions demand prompt treatment.

3rd. Every mother should know that an English mustard bath— hot—is the first resort in convulsions.

4th. While this is being done she can read the home treatment in this book and carry it out before the doctor comes.

5th. If the fit is not caused by some stomach or intestinal trouble, have the physician find out the cause and tell you what to do, and do it faithfully, because if you neglect the proper treatment the child may become idiotic or paralyzed.

BED WETTING. ENURESIS—INCONTINENCE

Enuresis, or incontinence of urine, is customary in infancy. Just when urination becomes a voluntary act depends upon the development and training of the individual child. As a rule children can be taught to control this function during the day, or while awake, about the tenth month. It is not under control during sleep until a much later period, usually by the end of the second year, but lack of control should not be regarded as abnormal until the child has entered the fourth year. If the child fails to control the act of urination during the day at the end of the second year, and is addicted to habitual bed-wetting, some measures should be adopted to cure the condition.

Boys under twelve years of age seem to be affected more frequently than girls. It is wrong to assume that it is caused by negligence or laziness, as some parents do. It has generally a special cause, and the cause usually can be found if it is carefully sought for. It may be the result of bad habits: exposure to cold in the night; lying on the back; drinking too much liquid in the afternoon or at bedtime. It may be due to too much acid in the urine, and if so it will be found necessary to reduce meats and eggs the child is eating. Worms, stone in the bladder, some anatomical abnormality or deficiency, may [581] be responsible for it. The diet may be at fault; adenoids are supposed by some physicians to be the cause. No matter what the actual cause may be, it must be found and remedied before we can hope for a permanent cure. A very large majority of these cases are due to nervousness. These children are of a nervous temperament. They are not necessarily sickly children; they are simply of a nervous type. They are well-nourished, active, and lively. Incontinence of urine during the day and long-continued bed-wetting does not at all affect the health of the child. If they are in poor health, it is essential to treat their general condition before trying to cure the incontinence.

It is absolutely wrong to punish or to crush the spirit of these children. Constant nagging and taunting, even if done in the hope of shaming the child into a cure, will simply make a coward of him and will not aid in improving matters, but will be distinctly detrimental.

Scrupulous cleanliness must be constantly practiced or these children, if neglected, may develop ulcers and sores of a very obstinate character. The odor is also bad for the health of the child.

Treatment.—Find and remove the cause if possible. If due to general poor health, give tonics, obtain a change of air, and build the child up. Reduce the total quantity of liquids, if in excess, and be very careful not to give any liquids near bedtime. Don't cover these children too much; they should never be "too warm"; they should sleep in a well-aired room, and they should receive a quick, cool sponge bath every morning. They should be taught to sleep on their sides, never on their backs. Their diet should be light but nourishing. When bed-wetting is established it will continue, if untreated, until the child is eight or ten years of age, and it frequently lasts much longer. When treatment is undertaken it should be distinctly understood by the mother that it will take many months to cure; and during these months she must give her constant attention to the child. If she does not undertake to do this, or if she fails to do it, the treatment should not be begun at all, as it will not succeed. Various plans should be tried to keep the child from sleeping on [582] its back. The reason of this is because it has been found that the child wets the bed only when sleeping on its back and never when sleeping on its side. The simplest method, of tying a towel or cloth around the child with a knot over the spinal column, so that it will hurt and waken it, if it turns on its back, is a very good one and should be carefully tried for some time. The nervous system of these children should never be overtaxed at home or at school. Early hours and plenty of sleep are desirable. Certain articles of diet of a stimulating character should be entirely avoided,—for example, coffee, tea, beer, candies, sugars, and pickles. The best diet for these children is one composed exclusively of milk, vegetables, fruits, meats, and cereals. Meats, however, should be given only once every two days. It is a good plan to teach the child to hold his water during the day, as long as he can, to accustom the bladder to being full. Adenoid growths, which contribute to the nervousness of a naturally nervous child, should be removed. It is a good plan to take the child up when the parents go in bed and let him urinate. This often cures the condition in itself.

Sometimes moral measures, such as the promise of a reward, will strengthen the will so that the child may overcome the tendency. Find out what the child most desires in the way of a toy, and promise it if he goes so long without wetting the bed. Aid and encourage him to make efforts to win the reward.

If drugs have to be resorted to, it is necessary to call the family physician, as the only drugs that are of any use are very powerful and have to be given with great care and caution. It is the experience of most physicians and specialists, however, that in a large majority of cases the treatment, along the lines as given above, will be effective, without drugs, if faithfully persisted in by the mother.

These children should be examined by a physician. The cause of the bed-wetting is frequently discovered to be produced by anatomical abnormalities which render circumcision imperative. In these cases no method of treatment will succeed until circumcision is performed. [583]

SLEEPLESSNESS. DISTURBED SLEEP

Causes.—In babies, disturbed sleep is most frequently due to hunger or to indigestion. The latter is the result of overfeeding or improper feeding. Rocking the child to sleep, or feeding it during the night will cause sleeplessness. Teething, colic, or any pain will result in disturbed sleep. Nervous children are frequently poor sleepers.

In older children, some digestive disturbance is, as a rule, the cause. Chronic intestinal indigestion, worms, adenoid growths, enlarged tonsils, lack of fresh air in the bedroom, cold feet, may, however, be the cause. Overstudy in school, poor blood, poor nourishment are always accompanied by inability to sleep soundly. Too strenuous play, exciting stories read before bedtime, may cause sleeplessness.

Treatment.—The removal of the cause is absolutely necessary. In order to discover the cause it is sometimes essential to study the child's whole routine in order to be able to tell exactly just what is causing the apparent insomnia. It may be necessary to change the method of feeding, to regulate the studies and the exercises, and to suggest changes regarding the sanitary and hygienic environment of the child's life. Mothers must be warned against using drugs in the form of soothing syrups or teething mixtures. They are dangerous and absolutely forbidden under the above conditions.

The nervous disposition of the child must be taken into consideration and treated if necessary. If bad habits exist they must be stopped. Poor blood and poor nutrition must receive the treatment suggested under these headings.

NIGHTMARE. NIGHT TERRORS

In a nightmare a child wakes suddenly in a state of fright and will inform you that it has had a bad dream. His mind seems clear and he recognizes those about him. He is not easily calmed and may cry for some time; finally he goes to sleep again. The next day he will remember [584] the dream and most of the incidents of the night before. Such cases are quite frequent. They are to be treated in the same way as cases of disturbed sleep, as they really have the same cause. They are mostly due to digestive disturbances and errors of diet.

Night-Terrors.—Cases under this heading form a distinct group by themselves. They are not frequent, but the condition is much more serious. The cause seems to be wholly nervous and may indicate an important nervous derangement. It seems to have some indefinite relation to such conditions as migraine, hysteria, epilepsy, and even insanity. The child wakes suddenly during the night and sits up, evidently in terror; he does not apparently regain his full consciousness. He talks of being scared, calls for his mother, trembles and shakes, cannot answer questions intelligently, and after a time goes to sleep. Next day he remembers nothing of the attack and does not seem to suffer in any way as a result of it.

I am disposed to believe that all of these attacks are not due to a nervous condition. A number of them of exactly this type have been cured by absolutely withdrawing milk from the diet.

It is a good plan to restrict the possibility of excessive play in these children. They are of the type whose play is work, and too much of it is too exhausting. Some person should sleep in the same room with these patients or in an adjoining room with the door open.

If the condition occurs frequently the child should be subjected to a thorough physical examination, because it may be one evidence of a serious ailment.

Sometimes these little patients have to be taken out of school and sent to the country, where they should remain for many months. It is far better to regard the condition as indicating an abnormality,—even though it may not have any deeper significance than that the digestive apparatus of the child is not quite right,—and make every effort to cure it, than to permit the child to go on under what really are unjust and unfavorable conditions. [585]

HEADACHE

Headaches are not common in little children. The most frequent ones are caused by:

1. Chronic indigestion and constipation.
2. Anemia and malnutrition.
3. Nervous disorders.
4. Diseases of the eye, nose, throat.
5. Rheumatism and gout.
6. Disturbances of the genital tract.

Those arising from anemia and poor nutrition are most frequently present in girls from ten to fifteen years of age. They may result from overcrowding of school work, which results in loss of appetite and poor sleep.

Nervous headaches may be hereditary or acquired through unhygienic surroundings. Hysteria, epilepsy, disease of the brain, neuralgia from carious teeth, may result in nervous headaches.

Headaches from disturbances of the genital tract may afflict girls about the time of puberty.

Treatment.—To remove the cause is the only plan that promises any result. Each one must be investigated by itself and dealt with accordingly. For the headache itself a hot foot bath, cold to the head, and small doses of phenacetine (one grain every hour for four doses) are perhaps the most certain of all methods of treatment.

THUMB-SUCKING

The habit of sucking the thumb may be corrected by wearing a pair of white mittens, or gloves tied at the wrist. Should children attempt to suck the thumb with gloves on, as some do, it will be necessary to saturate the thumb and fingers of the gloves with tincture of aloes, or a solution of the bisulphate of quinine, one dram to two ounces of water.

BITING THE FINGER NAILS

Biting the finger nails may be stopped by the use of the same bitter remedies as are used in thumb-sucking. [586]

HOW TO WASH OUT THE BOWELS

COLON IRRIGATION. A HIGH ENEMA

Procure a soft rubber catheter,—No. 18 American is about right. It is not advisable to get too soft rubber for the reason that it will buckle when the child strains and it will be impossible to wash out the bowel. Fill half full an ordinary two-quart douche bag with water that is warm, but not too hot. Dissolve a heaping teaspoonful of table salt in a glass of hot water and add this to the water in the bag. Hang the bag about two feet above the level of the child, so that the water will not flow in with too strong a stream; otherwise the child will immediately try to eject it. If the water flows in gently, the child may not object to it to the extent of making strenuous efforts to force the catheter out.

Use the small sized nozzle that comes with the douche bag. Place the rubber catheter over this nozzle, lubricate the catheter, place the child on its back over a douche pan, insert the catheter about two inches, let the water run and as it runs in push the catheter up gently until it is all in the bowel except the end on the douche tip. The object of letting the water run while pushing in the catheter is because it floats up with the water as it distends the bowel; there is no risk then of pushing the end into the intestinal wall or hurting the child. While the water is flowing into the bowel it is a good plan to compress the buttocks together to aid in holding the water, as the child is very apt to let it run out as soon as it feels uncomfortable.

The temperature of the water for the ordinary rectal injection should be 95° F. When the child is exhausted or very weak, or when the circulation is poor, the temperature of the water may be as high as 110° F. When, on the other hand, the fever is very high, the water may be much cooler; as low as 70° F. has been given with good results on the fever. If the irrigation is given with the intention of reducing the fever, it is best to begin with water around 90° F., and reduce it to 70° F., gradually. [587]

Indications for Irrigation of the Colon.—When it is desired to cleanse the bowel of any collection of matter a colon irrigation is indicated. This matter may be mucus, fecal substance, undigested food, or the decomposing waste products which may remain there as a result of disease or other conditions.

When it is desired to medicate by putting fluids into the bowel we adopt the colon infusion.

Every diseased condition of the bowel does not, however, indicate irrigation. If a child is having frequent loose movements every half-hour it is safe to assume that the bowel is being cleaned out sufficiently without any artificial aid. To irrigate in these cases would only irritate and would not accomplish anything. The cases which are benefited are those in which we have a fever with four or five green stools in the twenty-four hours, or where we have a high fever with no movement at all. To irrigate in these cases we not only get rid of the products of decomposition, but we prevent further decomposition and we reduce the fever, thereby contributing to the general welfare of the child.

When the child is convalescing and when there is only mucus in the stools, with no fever—as in cases of chronic ileo-colitis—the colon irrigations should be stopped, as they tend to keep up the discharge of mucus in these cases. If, however, there is a relapse with fever, which would indicate a fresh infection with more discharging mucus and possibly green stools, the irrigation must be used until the fever subsides.

Colon irrigations should always be given in every case of convulsions in infancy, first to clean out the bowel to prevent putrefaction, and second to empty the bowel on general principles because an overloaded bowel is very frequently the cause of convulsions in children.

When irrigation of the bowel is given at all it must be given thoroughly. Enough water must pass into the bowel to wash it all out. For this reason it is essential that the catheter should be all in and in the bowel—not doubled on itself two or three inches in the bowel. If it is a serious case and the mother nervous, someone else should give the washing—preferably the physician himself. [588] If the child objects strenuously, as often happens, it must be done with greater care to be successful. Remember that a colon irrigation is never given unless it is absolutely necessary and as a consequence it is given to accomplish a certain purpose; it must, therefore, be done thoroughly. If it is not, your child may miss the chance it has of getting over some immediate difficulty and if the moment of the "chance" is wasted or lost, that moment will not return. Be thorough, therefore.

Enema.—Some physicians talk about a high enema and a low enema. A high enema is really an irrigation as described above. The following remarks apply to low enemas only.

A so-called low enema is given to clean out the rectum of constipated matter, or for the introduction of food or medicine by rectum, when for various reasons it is necessary to spare the stomach.

It may be given with the fountain syringe or with the ordinary bulb (baby) syringe. A catheter may be put on the tip of the syringe if it is thought best to inject higher up than in the rectum.

When an enema is used in infants or older children for the relief of constipation, the best medium to use is glycerine. For an infant, one teaspoonful to an ounce of water is sufficient; for older children, one tablespoonful to two ounces of water, given with the bulb syringe, will give prompt results. If the constipation is pronounced, the fecal mass very hard, an enema of sweet oil, allowed to remain in for ten minutes, will soften it and permit a movement.

Soap suds are often used. They are good but not as reliable as the glycerine or oil; if, however, neither of these two are at hand the soap suds may be given.

Enemas should be carefully given and the liquid slowly injected. If the fountain syringe is used care must be exercised in not having the bag too high. If it is too high the liquid will flow in too strongly, either injuring the bowel wall or causing the child to strain immediately and pass out the injection before it has an opportunity of accomplishing its work. [589]

The temperature of the enema should be warm—not hot, and not cold, simply body heat.

METHODS OF REDUCING FEVER

During the course of acute illness it is frequently necessary to reduce the fever, if possible, without the use of drugs. The following means are often adopted. It is desirable that the mother should know just how to carry out these methods:

Ice-Cap.—An ice-cap is used to protect the brain when a child or adult is running a very high fever. It is put on when the fever is above 103° F. It may be used in other conditions—brain disease, or disease of the meninges or cord—in which case the physician will be in attendance and will direct what should be done.

Ice-bags are procured in the drug stores. The best one is the flat French ice-bag. Fill it three-quarters full of finely chopped ice, put the ice-bag in a towel, and place on the patient's head. There should be only one thickness of the towel between the ice-bag and the head.

It will be necessary to keep a record of the fever so that the ice-bag may be withdrawn when it falls below 103° F.

When the ice melts the bag must be at once refilled. This is often overlooked by careless mothers.

Cold Sponging.—Cold sponging is used to reduce fever or to allay nervous irritability. Equal parts of alcohol and water or vinegar and water are used. The temperature of the water should be 80° to 85° F.

Infants to be sponged should be completely undressed and laid upon a blanket. The sponging should be done for about fifteen or twenty minutes, after which the child is wrapped in a dry blanket without further clothing except the diaper. To be effective it must be done frequently.

Cold Pack.—The cold pack is used to reduce fever. It is one of the simplest and one of the best means we have. The child is undressed completely, and laid upon a blanket. It is completely covered with a small blanket (except its head) wrung out of water at 100° F. Outside [590] of this the child is rubbed with a piece of ice, front and back, for a sufficiently long time to render the surface cool, but not cold. Children take kindly to this means of reducing fever; there is no shock and they are quieted by it.

Just how long one will rub with the ice depends upon circumstances. From five to thirty minutes may be employed. The head should be sponged with cold water while this is being done and it is a good plan to have a hot-water bottle at the child's feet.

The Cold Bath.—To reduce fever the cold bath is used in the following way: Water at a temperature of 100° F. is put into the bath and the child is first put into this water, then the water is reduced by putting into it shaved ice until it reaches 80° F. The child's body is well rubbed while it is in the bath and cold water is applied to its head. The bath is continued for five minutes, or sometimes with a robust child to ten minutes. On removal the child should be put into a warm blanket after being thoroughly dried.

Rectal Irrigations.—These are sometimes given to reduce fever. They are very useful and very successful if they are given properly and without exciting the child too much. It is best to give water of an ordinary temperature at first and gradually reduce it to 70° F. It should be continued for ten minutes or longer. It may be repeated every three hours. (See page 586.)

VARIOUS BATHS

Every mother should know how to give any bath that may be directed by the physician.

The Mustard Bath.—Take from three to four tablespoonfuls of English mustard; mix thoroughly in about one gallon of warm water. Add to this about five gallons of plain water at a temperature of 100° F. If it is necessary to raise the temperature of the water higher it may be done by adding water until the temperature reaches 105° or 110° F.

The mustard bath is exceedingly effective in cases of shock, great sudden depression, collapse, heart failure, [591] or in sudden congestion of the lungs or brain. The special use of the mustard bath is in the treatment of convulsions; it is also useful for nervous children who sleep badly. Two or three minutes in the mustard bath, followed by a quick rubbing, will induce refreshing sleep in these children. It is not necessary to have more than one tablespoonful of mustard in these cases.

The Hot Bath.—A bath is prepared of water at a temperature of 100° F. After the child is in the bath the temperature of the water is raised to 105°, or to 110° F. It is not safe to go above this point.

The body of the child should be well rubbed while it is in the bath. In most cases it is advisable to apply cold water to the head while the child is in the bath. A bath thermometer should be kept in the water to see that it does not rise above the temperature desired.

The hot bath, like the mustard bath, is used to promote reaction in cases of shock, collapse, etc., and in convulsions.

The Hot Pack.—Remove all clothing from the baby and envelop the body in a sheet wrung out of water at a temperature of 100° F., to 105° F., after which the body should be rolled in a thick blanket. Those hot applications may be changed every twenty minutes until free perspiration is produced. This condition may be kept up as long as is necessary.

The hot pack is used mainly in disease of the kidney.

The Hot-Air or Vapor Bath.—The child is put in bed wholly undressed with the bedclothing raised about twelve inches, and held in that position by a wicker support. The child's head is of course outside the bed clothing. Beneath the bed clothing hot air or vapor from a croup kettle is introduced. This will cause free perspiration in twenty minutes. It may be continued from twenty to thirty minutes at a time.

The vapor bath is used in diseases of the kidney, as a rule.

The Bran Bath.—In five gallons of water place a bag in which is put one quart of ordinary wheat bran. The bag is made of cheese cloth. Squeeze and manipulate the bran bag until the water resembles a thin porridge. [592] The temperature of the water is usually about 95° F., though it may be given with any temperature of water.

The bran bath is of great value in eczema, or in rashes about the buttocks, or in delicate skin conditions when plain water would irritate.

The Tepid Bath.—This bath may be given at a temperature of 95°, or 100° F. It is of distinct advantage in extremely nervous children. To induce sleep it is often better than drugs.

The Cold Sponge or Shower Bath.—This bath should be given in the morning in a warm room. A tub should be provided with enough water in it to cover the child's feet. This water should be warm because when the feet are in warm water it prevents the shock which frequently comes when cold water is applied to any other part of the body.

A large sponge is filled with water at a temperature of from 40° to 60° F. This is squeezed a number of times over the child's chest, shoulders, and back. While the cold water is being applied the body should be well rubbed with the free hand of the mother. The bath should not last longer than half a minute. When finished take the child out quickly and stand him on a bath towel and give him a brisk rubbing with a bath towel until the skin reacts. This is an exceedingly valuable tonic for a delicate child. It should not be used on younger children than eighteen months of age. In younger children a cold plunge is preferable.

For the cold plunge water at a temperature of 55° F. is prepared. The child is lifted into this and given a single dip up to the neck. He is then briskly rubbed off as above.

There are a very few children who do not take kindly to either the cold sponge or plunge. These children do not react; they remain pale or blue and pinched for some time after. It may be necessary to discontinue the procedure or to use water of a higher temperature.

POULTICES

Poultices are useful in inflammation and for the relief of pain. To be of any value they should be applied [593] frequently—every ten or twenty minutes—and they should be applied hot.

Ground flaxseed is the best material for poultices. It should be mixed with boiling water until the proper thickness is reached. It may be kept simmering on a fire. When one poultice is taken off it can be scraped into the pot and heated over if there is no discharge. Each poultice should be put into clean muslin, put on the part and covered with oiled silk. This will help to retain the heat and prevent the clothing or bed sheet from becoming wet.

HOT FOMENTATIONS

A hot fomentation is simply a clean poultice. Several thicknesses of flannel are taken, wrung out of very hot water, covered with cotton batting, and then with oiled silk.

How to Make and How to Apply a Mustard Paste.—For infants: Take one part English mustard to six parts flour, mix with lukewarm water, and spread between two layers of cheesecloth.

For older children and adults: Take one tablespoonful English mustard to three or four tablespoonfuls of flour, and mix as above.

Mustard pastes should be made big enough. You can accomplish a great deal more by putting on a sufficiently large mustard paste than by simply putting on one the size of the palm of your hand.

It should be left on until the skin is distinctly red. The length of time will depend, of course, upon the strength of the mustard. Mustard pastes may be put on every three hours, if necessary, and they may be used for a week at this interval if the conditions demand it.

If they are used in pneumonia or other pulmonary diseases, they should be used large enough to go around the whole chest. If they are used in heart failure, they should be big enough to cover the whole trunk.

When made with the white of an egg they will not blister. Or if the part is rubbed with white vaseline before applying, it will not blister and it will be just as [594] effective. When a mustard paste is removed the red area should be rubbed with white vaseline and covered with a clean piece of flannel.

How to Prepare and Use the Mustard Pack.—The child is stripped and laid upon a blanket, and the trunk is surrounded by a large towel or sheet saturated with mustard water. This is prepared as follows: Take one tablespoonful of English mustard and dissolve it in one quart of water, slightly warmed. Saturate a towel in this mixture and apply to the body of the child while it is dripping. The patient is then rolled in a blanket. Keep the child in this pack for ten or fifteen minutes. The mustard pack is not as good as the mustard bath, but it is all that is necessary in a number of various conditions. The physician will, of course, decide these matters. It is simply the duty of the mother to know how to carry out the physician's instructions.

The Turpentine Stupe.—Take a piece of flannel, big enough to cover the area which it is desired to affect, wring it out of as hot water as it is possible. Upon this sprinkle twenty drops of spirits of turpentine. Place the stupe wherever it is desired and cover with a piece of oiled silk or dry flannel. The turpentine stupe is mostly used in pain of the abdominal cavity. In colic from acute indigestion it is a very convenient means of quieting the child by allaying the pain.

Care should be taken not to allow this form of application to remain on too long. Take it off when the skin is red. For continuous use it is not as good as the mustard paste.

OILED SILK. WHAT IT IS, AND WHY IT IS USED

Oiled silk is sold in the drug stores by the yard. It is one yard wide. It is used to cover any local application to prevent evaporation into the air or to prevent the clothing from absorbing the medicament. If a liniment is applied on cloth to effect a certain result, it may take some time to do its work. If the wet cloth is covered with the clothing, the clothing will absorb the medicine quicker than the body will and thereby defeat the object [595] in view, in addition to rendering the clothing wet and nasty. If the application is covered with oiled silk it cannot escape into the clothing, because the oiled silk is impervious. The body will be compelled to absorb the medicine and consequently results will be quicker and more certain. Many liniments are expensive; to permit them to be absorbed by the clothing is needless waste It is therefore economical to apply the oiled silk.

[596]

DISEASES OF CHILDREN

[597]

By permission of Henry H. Goddard.

The First Blight

This is one of those truly unfortunate cases which, so far as present knowledge goes, cannot be guarded against. Eunice, age 31, mentally 2, is a low-grade imbecile. There is not in the whole family, for generations back, a single case of feeble-mindedness, nor of disease that would undermine the nervous organization. Close scrutiny does not reveal a single assignable cause. She came, as an accident, to blight an otherwise normal family.

Such cases are few, but unfortunately they do occur. It is for Eugenics to materially reduce the possibility of such occurrences.

[598]

[599]

CHAPTER XXXVIII

INFECTIOUS OR CONTAGIOUS DISEASES

Rules to be Observed in the Treatment of Contagious Diseases—What Isolation Means—The Contagious Sick Room—Conduct and Dress of the Nurse—Feeding the Patient and Nurse—How to Disinfect the Clothing and Linen—How to Disinfect the Urine and Feces—How to Disinfect the Hands—Disinfection of the Room Necessary—How to Disinfect the Mouth and Nose—How to Disinfect the Throat— Receptacle for the Sputum—Care of the Skin in Contagious Diseases—Convalescence After a Contagious Disease—Disinfecting the Sick Chamber—The After Treatment of a Disinfected Room— How to Disinfect the Bed Clothing and Clothes—Mumps—Epidemic Parotitis—Chicken Pox—Varicella—La Grippe— Influenza—Diphtheria—Whooping Cough—Pertussis— Measles—Koplik's Spots—Department of Health Rules in Measles—Scarlet Fever—Scarlatina—Typhoid Fever— Various Solutions—Boracic Acid Solution—Normal Salt Solution—Carron Oil—Thiersch's Solution—Solution of Bichloride of Mercury—How to Make Various Solutions.

RULES TO BE OBSERVED IN THE TREATMENT OF CONTAGIOUS DISEASES

Every mother should know the elementary principles involved in the treatment of contagious diseases. They are contagious because they may be conveyed from one individual to another or because a person nursing a victim of a contagious disease may carry that disease to another person without having the disease herself. For this reason, certain rules have been established by the medical profession, which experience has taught are necessary in order to preserve the health of the community when such diseases are prevalent.

The very first rule to which the physician will direct the mother's attention, when there is a contagious disease, will be that the child must be "isolated."

What Isolation Means.—Isolation means the complete seclusion of the patient in a room by himself, so that [600] no one will see him or come in contact with him except the physician and the nurse or mother who will tend him during the entire course of the disease. Isolation implies more than it would seem to mean. It implies that every article used during the sickness will be thoroughly disinfected before it leaves the room in which the patient himself is isolated. Mothers must always remember that every article used by the patient may carry the germs of the disease to some other member of the family or to some other individual. These articles are the clothing of the child, the bedclothes, napkins, handkerchiefs, towels, dishes, knives and spoons, rags, the various discharges—sputum, urine, and bowel passages—and, we may add to this list, flies, insects, and domestic animals. Every precaution must, therefore, be taken to safeguard any dissemination of the disease by means of these articles.

Thorough isolation also implies that the nurse shall frequently bathe and disinfect her person and her clothing, and that the sick-room itself shall be carefully dusted with a moist cloth and disinfected from time to time.

The Contagious Sick-Room.—The contagious sick-room will be prepared in exactly the same way as the ordinary sick-room which has been previously described. In addition, however, it will be safeguarded in the following manner. A wet sheet will be hung up outside the door. This sheet will be kept constantly moistened with a solution of chloride of lime. One-half pound to an ordinary house-pail of water is the strength of the solution to use. Every window must be effectively screened to prevent the ingress and egress of flies and other insects.

Conduct and Dress of the Nurse.—She will remain in the sick-room all the time unless when she takes outdoor exercise. Her dress will consist of a long gown which will entirely cover her person from the neck to the shoes and will be of plain, white, easily washed material, without tucks or ruffles or adornment of any kind. She should wear an ordinary pair of house slippers made of light leather. Her cap will be large enough [601] to cover and include her hair and head. When she leaves the room, she will remove her cap, gown, and slippers, disinfect her hands in a disinfecting solution and wash her face, neck, and hands in soap and water. She should go directly out and in, without coming in contact with any occupant of the home.

Feeding the Patient and Nurse.—The meals for the patient and nurse should be left on a table outside the door of the sick-room, from which place the nurse will then take them into the room. The utensils used for these meals should not be used by other members of the family during the entire sickness. After the patient and nurse have eaten, the utensils should be placed in a chloride of lime solution for disinfection. If any of the food is left over it should be put into a jar in which it may be disinfected and rendered harmless before being disposed of.

How to Disinfect the Clothing and Linen.—All bed and body linen, towels, handkerchiefs, napkins, etc., should be immediately put into a large receptacle—a wash boiler, or tub, will answer the purpose admirably—containing a five per cent. solution of carbolic acid in which an adequate quantity of soft soap has been dissolved. They should remain in this mixture for two hours, after which they may be wrung out and taken to the laundry.

How to Disinfect the Urine and Feces.—The urine and the stools should be passed into vessels containing a solution of four ounces of carbolic acid to the gallon of water. This vessel should be covered and the mixture allowed to stand for one hour, after which time it may be thrown out.

How to Disinfect the Hands.—Any of the following solutions may be used for disinfection of the nurse's hands: Creolin, one teaspoonful to the quart of water; chloride of lime, one-half pound to a pail of water; formalin, thirty-two drops to a quart of water. A basin containing one of the above solutions should be constantly kept standing for the frequent disinfection of the nurse's hands. After disinfection, the hands should be washed in plain water and soap. [602]

Disinfection of Room Necessary.—The room in which a contagious patient is confined requires systematic attention on the part of the nurse. Every other day all flat or projecting surfaces should be disinfected. Mantels, window-sills, door knobs, picture moldings, furniture, chairs, and bed-railings, should be wiped with cloths moistened in a disinfecting solution. A suitable solution for this purpose is one containing one ounce of carbolic acid to the quart of water.

How to Disinfect the Mouth and Nose.—In the course of all contagious diseases the mouth and throat of the patient and nurse should be thoroughly disinfected as a matter of routine. It should be done at least twice daily unless more frequent disinfection is called for because of the nature of the disease. In measles and diphtheria, for example, the nasal and throat conditions will undoubtedly call for more frequent and more thorough disinfection than twice daily. This may also apply to scarlet fever if the throat is involved as is often the case.

Pocket handkerchiefs should never be used by a patient suffering from a contagious disease. The nose and mouth should be wiped with pieces of gauze or cheesecloth, cut into small squares for this purpose. These should be immediately burned after being used.

To disinfect the throat, a solution of formalin, six drops to six ounces of water, is effective. To disinfect the nose, a solution of Glyco-Thymoline is suitable. These applications should be made by means of an atomizer, a different atomizer being used for the patient and nurse.

Receptacle for the Sputum.—A cuspidor, or basin, should be constantly kept at the side of the bed in which the patient may conveniently expectorate. This utensil should contain the chloride of lime solution previously mentioned.

Care of the Skin in Contagious Diseases.—As in all other sick conditions, the skin of the patient should be bathed frequently with an alcoholic solution. In the later stages of measles and scarlet fever it is essential to anoint the skin while the patient is scaling. This may be done with carbolated vaseline. Mothers should [603] understand why this is necessary. These diseases have a distinct rash or eruption. This eruption practically kills the skin cells and at a certain period these cells are cast off by the new growth of skin underneath. This process is called scaling. In measles the scales are small, and are cast off in the form of bran like dust. In scarlet fever, the cells adhere together and are cast off in large scales. These scales are contagious. They are very light and will float in the air if dry. The movement of the patient, changing the bed clothing, etc., will waft a multitude of these contagious scales into the air of the room and infect every article they may land on. This would make the disinfection of the room difficult and tedious. In order to obviate this tendency experience has taught us that much of the difficulty and nearly all of the risk of contagion may be overcome by rubbing some oily or sticky substance on the skin. By this method the dust and scales are rendered heavier than the air, stick together and will not float. During the scaling period there is a constant itch present which irritates the little patient. By using carbolated vaseline to anoint the skin we accomplish two purposes. The carbolic acid in the vaseline relieves the itch, and the vaseline itself greases the skin so that the scales remain in the bed. Each day the nurse changes the bed-sheet, gathers the scales in the sheet and puts all in the disinfecting solution.

Convalescence After a Contagious Disease.—Complete isolation must be kept up until all danger from contagion is passed. In diphtheria this period is not reached until the examination of the throat contents under the microscope is returned negative. In diseases which have a rash this period is not reached until all scaling is completed. Even then, and for a number of days or weeks, the patient may be taken out for exercise daily, but must not be allowed to play with other children until his strength justifies active exercise. It takes a much longer period to rid the system of the poison of a contagious disease than most mothers appreciate. Many children have died from heart failure after they were considered well simply because the active [604] exercise overtaxed the heart before the system was wholly free from the poison of the disease.

Before the child is removed from the sick-room for the first time he should have a disinfecting bath. This bath should be in a solution of bichloride of mercury, the strength of which should be one part to five thousand parts of water. The towels used to dry the patient after the bath should be fresh and should not have been in the sick-room. He should then be dressed in clothing which has never been in the sick-room.

DISINFECTING THE SICK-CHAMBER

How to Disinfect a Room.—The most efficient way to disinfect a room is by means of formaldehyde gas. This, however, requires a special apparatus which can only be used by one familiar with the process. In all large cities the Department of Health usually undertakes the disinfection of rooms after any contagious disease. The next best method is by sulphur.

When sulphur is employed it should be used in the form of powder or in small pieces. This is placed in a shallow iron pan set on a couple of boards in a tub partly filled with water. The sulphur is moistened with alcohol before it is set on fire.

It is always necessary, of course, before disinfecting by any process to make the room as nearly air tight as is possible. To accomplish this the windows must be tightly closed, the doors locked, and the cracks and keyhole sealed with pieces of paper or adhesive paper. The room should remain closed for six or eight hours, after which it should be thoroughly aired for several days.

The After Treatment of a Disinfected Room.—The walls, ceiling, and all flat surfaces, such as mantels, window-sills, etc., should be washed with a fresh chloride of lime solution. The floor should be scrubbed with a four per cent. soda solution. All carpets and curtains, if any, should be removed, taken to a vacant lot and thoroughly beaten and then exposed to direct sunlight for a number of hours. The room should then be well aired again for a couple of days before it is again occupied. [605]

How to Disinfect the Bed Clothing and Clothes.—The surest way is to boil them for half an hour; otherwise they may be left in the room while it is being disinfected. Spraying the clothes with a spray of formaldehyde is an effective way of disinfecting them.

MUMPS: EPIDEMIC PAROTITIS

Mumps is a contagious disease. It is most common between the fourth and sixth years. Infants are rarely affected. The disease is not very contagious, direct contact being necessary to communicate it. Every case should be isolated for a period of three weeks from the beginning of the disease.

The seat of the affection is the parotid gland which is located in front of and on a level with the ear. One or both glands may be affected at the same time or one may follow the other in succumbing. The duration of the disease from the time the swelling becomes noticeable is about ten days. It is contagious for a week after the swelling subsides. The period of incubation is from one to three weeks.

Symptoms.—In the majority of cases the first symptom is the swelling and the discomfort which it causes. In more severe cases the child feels sick and is listless for from twenty-four to forty-eight hours. There may be a headache, vomiting, pains in the back and limbs, and fever. There is pain in the swelling which is increased by movement of the jaws and by pressure. The degree of the swelling varies with the severity of the attack. It may be very little or it may be so great as to completely distort, and render unrecognizable, the face. It must be remembered that, though mumps is not regarded as an important or dangerous disease, it may assume dangerous characteristics.

We sometimes see distressing complications with mumps. In boys, orchitis, or inflammation of the testicles, occasionally occur. In girls, ovaritis, or inflammation of the ovaries may be present. These complications may be avoided by keeping the patients in bed.

Treatment.—Keep the child in bed until the fever is [606] gone. Keep him in the house for one week after the swelling has entirely subsided. He should be put on a liquid diet while the fever lasts. The bowels should move each day.

The mouth should be kept clean by an antiseptic mouth wash. If there is much pain in the swollen gland, warm, wet dressings give the best results. Sometimes it is advisable to paint the gland with belladonna ointment. If it is not very painful, the most comfortable way to dress the gland is simply to place over it a large pad of absorbent cotton held in place by a broad strip of flannel cloth.

CHICKEN POX. VARICELLA

Chicken pox is an affection almost entirely special to children, in whom it may be observed from their first year, although it is especially frequent from the ages of two to six. It appears often in the epidemical form and spreads by contagion.

Some doctors are inclined to regard varicella as a very attenuated form of smallpox, hence the name "chicken pox," by which it is popularly known. This opinion is based merely on the analogy between the two types of skin eruptions and the coincidence sometimes observed between two epidemics of smallpox and chicken pox. But the theory falls on considering that, on the one hand, chicken pox offers no safeguard against infection by smallpox and does not prevent the effects of vaccination, and, on the other hand the disease may occur in children who have been vaccinated or who have had smallpox. Chicken pox, too, differs essentially from smallpox in the course of its development.

After a period of incubation, extending over a fortnight, chicken pox becomes apparent by such symptoms as slight shivering, extreme fatigue and a general but not very intense condition of fever. In less than twenty-four hours small pink spots will appear on the skin, and these after a few hours are topped by a vesicle, and the next day the whole rash shows a vesiculous appearance.

The vesicles are sometimes small and pointed, sometimes more voluminous and globular in form. They [607] are filled with a limpid or a slightly yellowish liquid. Their base is sometimes surrounded by an inflammatory ring. By the third day the contents of the vesicle has become thicker and tends to become purulent. On the fourth day desiccation commences, and the vesicles shrivel and shrink in and form small brownish scabs, which fall about the eighth day. Frequently the child will scratch them off with the finger nails before they are entirely desiccated. The vesicles leave small reddish spots, which generally disappear gradually, almost always without a scar.

An eruption of chicken pox does not burst out all over the body at once, but appears in successive rashes. It is not confined to any special parts of the body. It may begin and spread at the same time from the face, the trunk of the body or the limbs. A dozen pimples may be seen the first day, while three or even ten times as many may be visible the next day, and so on for several days in succession.

Sometimes the vesicles appear on mucous membrane at different parts—the mouth, tongue, soft palate and tonsils—and may also invade the conjunctiva and cornea, or the larynx, where they will set up laryngitis.

Owing to the very contagious nature of chicken pox, the first thing to be done is to provide for the complete isolation during a period of twelve to fifteen days of all patients attacked by the disease.

The treatment of the disease is solely a matter of hygiene. The more severe the fever the stricter the diet should be, and in the case of great fever, the diet should be restricted to broth and milk. If there is no fever the child need not be placed on any special diet.

If the intestines are sluggish, they may be stimulated by administering a dose of castor oil. It is advisable to make the patient rinse his mouth two or three times a day with a mouth wash. It is also well to apply a lotion around the eyes and face, consisting of two per cent. boracic acid solution with the chill taken off. Finally, in order to prevent the child scratching the sores and the consequent danger of inoculation by the finger nails, it is a good practice to rub a small amount [608] of carbolated vaseline over the itching parts. It is frequently found necessary to have the little patient wear white woolen gloves to prevent scratching and infecting the sores. If a child scratches the sores on the face it will leave an unsightly mark which will stay for the rest of its life.

The child, of course, should not be allowed to rejoin his playmates without having had a good bath, and having had his clothes completely disinfected.

INFLUENZA: LA GRIPPE

The most important feature with reference to influenza in children is its very active tendency to develop complications. These complications generally affect the respiratory tract. So we find in children suffering from grippe an easy disposition to get bronchitis or broncho-pneumonia. The younger the child the greater the danger.

The disease itself, so long as it remains an uncomplicated influenza, is not of much importance or severity. The lesson to be learnt, therefore, is to treat the disease with respect and take every precaution to avoid the possibility of developing a complication.

La Grippe is a highly contagious disease. It prevails epidemically, and after an active epidemic it may remain in the vicinity for a number of years. It is more frequently seen in the late winter months and early spring. The poison of the disease clings to clothing and apartments as well as to railroad and street cars. The germ is found in the sputum and in the nasal secretions.

Sneezing is one of its symptoms and it is one of the ways by which the disease is spread around. Children should never be brought near an adult suffering from influenza. One attack does not render the patient immune to a subsequent attack as is the case with most of the contagious diseases. The reverse is the rule with La Grippe because one attack favors the development of another attack. It is a common experience for many people to have influenza every winter or spring.

Symptoms.—If a child "catches" grippe, it becomes [609] quite sick abruptly. There is usually chilliness, pains in the muscles all over the body, more or less fever, sometimes nausea and vomiting. If the attack is a more severe one, the prostration is more marked, the temperature higher and the signs of shock and poisoning of the system are more in evidence. A child a few months old can get influenza so severely as to cause collapse and death in thirty-six hours. As a rule the type of grippe most common in infancy is of a very mild character. It lasts about a week. Children may be a little slow in convalescing and it may be three or four weeks before they regain their health.

Complications.—As has been intimated, the most frequent complication is bronchitis and the most fatal one is broncho-pneumonia.

A congestion of the entire mucous membrane of the respiratory tract, producing a nasal discharge, a sore and inflamed throat, pains and a feeling of compression, with a cough in the chest, may accompany the disease.

Gastric symptoms, with vomiting, intestinal disturbance, diarrhea, with or without mucus and blood, are quite common in some epidemics.

Not infrequently we have numerous cases in which the ear seems to be the vulnerable part. As a consequence running ears have to receive most of our attention. When the ears are affected, the glands of the neck become inflamed. They swell up and add considerable to the discomfort of the little patient.

Treatment.—Cases of influenza should be isolated. Children should be put in a room by themselves and the other children of the family should not be permitted to see them. The rooms should be disinfected after the case is over. As complications are the dangerous element in grippe, we should try to prevent them. This can be best done by promptly putting the child in bed, making him comfortable, opening his bowels by castor oil or calomel. He should be made to drink hot lemonade. He should be kept on a light diet from which meat and vegetables are excluded.

The above treatment will usually suffice in the ordinary [610] uncomplicated grippe. If complications arise they must be treated according to the conditions.

It is well to remember that the degree of prostration following a rather severe attack of grippe is out of all proportion to the extent of the disease. These little patients sometimes suffer considerably and do not regain their strength promptly. Experience has taught us that the best thing to do is to send them away. A change of climate will do wonders for them, more quickly and more thoroughly than all the medicine we can give them at home. The seashore is particularly good for them.

DIPHTHERIA

Diphtheria is an acute, specific, infectious, communicable disease. It affects the tonsils, throat, nose, or larynx. It is most frequently seen in children between the ages of two and five years, though it may appear at any time during life. The two sexes are equally liable to it. The same person may have the disease twice or more times at different ages. Children suffering from disease of the nose or throat are more likely to get it than are others. Such diseases are cold in the head with running nose, catarrh of the nose and throat, inflammation of the mucous membranes of the nose or throat.

Diphtheria may occur at any time of the year, though it is more frequent during the cold months. The incubation, or the length of time between exposure to the disease and the development of the symptoms, is between two and five days. In its mild form the disease may be present without giving any constitutional symptoms. In its severe form, however, it is one of the most dangerous diseases of childhood. In large cities it is present all the year round with more or less frequent outbreaks in the form of local epidemics. In the country it is only seen in its epidemic form. It does not arise without a cause, that is, there is always a preceding case from which an epidemic springs, though it is not always easy to trace the connection. The child inhales the bacilli which cause the disease with the air it breathes. The [611] bacilli may lodge on toys or other articles from which the child gets them. Direct infection is usually the mode of communication through which a child obtains the disease. The saliva and mucus from the nose contain the bacilli in large quantities and if a patient coughs or sneezes they are expelled in this way and infect others. Frequently a child suffering from a mild form of diphtheria may attend school and infect others without it being known that the child has the disease.

Symptoms.—The symptoms vary with the severity of the attack. There are mild cases, as has been stated, that give no constitutional symptoms. There may be a small amount of local disturbance in the throat or nose and there may be some membrane present, but, for some reason, there does not seem to be any absorption of the poison into the system and the child escapes the systemic disturbance. Even as a local condition these cases vary. There is always a fever at the beginning, but the child never seems sick enough to go to bed. If the throat is examined it will be found to be red and slightly inflamed, there may be spots on the tonsils, or there may be a gray film over them. There is no discharge from the nose and the child does not complain of an excess of mucus from the throat. The spots may last for a week and then disappear. These cases are difficult to diagnose without making a culture, and if the physician insists upon keeping the child confined to bed while apparently well the family as a rule object, though it is absolutely necessary. These are the cases that do great harm in school, and no mother should object if the physician insists in taking preventative measures to stop an epidemic if the bacilli have been found in the child's throat. She should rather feel thankful that the child escaped so easily.

Since the introduction of antitoxin we do not see the severe cases now, so that a description of them would not be of any use in a book of this character. Mothers should, however, know that it is absolutely criminal to take any chances with a "sore throat."

Antitoxin is a prompt and an absolute remedy if used soon after the onset of the disease. It is more sure if used the first [612] or second day, still reliable the third day, but its efficacy diminishes the longer we postpone its use from the date of the onset of the disease. When, therefore, a child complains of being sick and states that its throat hurts, medical aid should be at once sought.

The disease may develop in one of two ways. It may begin as a slight indisposition for a day or two, and perhaps some soreness of the throat. The fever may be slight. The child will continue to be sick despite any treatment given and will get slowly worse until the fourth or fifth day, when it will be impossible to mistake the condition.

At other times the disease begins abruptly. The child complains of being sick. It may vomit, or suffer from headache, chilly feelings, and a fever. The glands in the neck may swell and cause considerable disturbance. There is, as a rule, an abundant discharge from the nose and there is an excess of mucus in the throat. Membrane is seen in the throat. It may cover the tonsils and spread over the entire throat cavity, or it may extend up into the nose and over the roof of the mouth. All the parts are much swollen and breathing is interfered with, sometimes seriously. If the attack is very severe there is an active absorption of poison going on from the throat which soon renders the little patient intensely sick. There is marked weakness and prostration, the circulation becomes poor, the pulse rapid and the child falls into a stupor.

The physician will, of course, have taken complete charge of the case before the patient has gone thus far. The nursing of the case, which may fall to the mother if no trained nurse is present, is most important. She should preserve absolute cleanliness of herself and of the sick room. She should never eat or sleep in the same room with the patient, and should use a gargle, which the physician should prescribe, frequently during the day. She should dress simply, so that whatever is worn can be changed often and washed easily. Every article of furniture must be taken out of the sick room that is not absolutely essential in the care of the case. If toys are allowed they should be burned as soon as [613] the child is tired of them, never left around the house after the case is over. The room should be a large one and it should be thoroughly aired each day. The floor should be washed each day with a solution of bichloride of mercury, and all dusting should be done with a wet cloth. The bed linen and any rags or handkerchiefs used should be treated as in scarlet fever. All vessels in which the patient expectorates should have an antiseptic in them. The room must be disinfected after the case is over.

The patient must be kept in bed during the entire attack. He must not be allowed to even sit up in bed until the physician gives him permission. This is a very important essential in the treatment of this disease, and the nurse must be held responsible for the conduct of the patient in this respect. Because of the character of the poison, there is a tendency to paralysis of the heart, and frequently children have been allowed to sit up too soon only to fall back dead in bed. The same thing has occurred later in the disease when children have been allowed to play too heartily before the poison had an opportunity to completely eliminate itself. Nursing children should be fed on breast milk pumped from the mother, but they must not nurse it themselves. Older children can take milk and should depend upon it mostly. The physician will give any other special directions that he may think necessary, the duty of the mother being to see that they are faithfully carried out.

WHOOPING-COUGH

Whooping-cough is usually seen in young children. It may, however, affect a person at any age. It is contagious. During infancy it is one of the most fatal diseases. During adult life it is a dangerous condition, while in childhood it is simply regarded as a mildly contagious disease.

It is most contagious during the catarrhal stage,—the first ten days. Children suffering from whooping-cough should not be allowed to mix or play with other children for two months. After an exposure to the [614] disease it takes about fourteen days for a case to develop. The danger of whooping-cough is the tendency to develop pneumonia or bronchitis.

Symptoms.—During the first ten days the child acts as if suffering from an ordinary catarrhal cold with cough. This is called the catarrhal stage. There is no way of telling that whooping-cough is present until the child whoops. Most children do not whoop until the expiration of the catarrhal stage, though a very few do from the beginning of the disease. If a child is treated for an ordinary cold with cough and does not respond to treatment, and whooping-cough is epidemic, it is fair to assume that whooping-cough has been contracted. When the cough shows a distinct tendency to be worse at night it is further proof of this assumption.

When they begin to cough in paroxysms, and whoop, the second, or spasmodic stage begins. These fits of paroxysmal coughing are much more severe than spells of ordinary coughing. These may only be three or four attacks daily, or the child may have from forty to fifty such attacks. When children feel these attacks coming on they seek support, holding on to chairs or they stand by the mother's knee. The coughing is explosive, rapid, and forceful, the child fails to catch its breath and is compelled to take a deep inspiration, which is the whoop; it then goes on coughing more. The face may become purple, the eyes protrude, and the veins of the face swell up. Near the end of the attack the child raises, or vomits a mass of stringy, glutinous mucus. After it is over the child is exhausted, there is a more or less profuse perspiration, and he may be quite dazed. These attacks are, as a rule, more frequent and more severe during the night. This stage lasts about one month and is then followed by the stage of decline, during which the disease subsides into what appears as an ordinary bronchial cold.

It is quite common for these children to get relapses, especially during inclement winter weather, and go on whooping for two or three months longer. Their vitality suffers because their sleep and nourishment is interfered with, and they become nervous and difficult to manage. [615]

Treatment.—Inasmuch as there is no remedy known that will cure whooping-cough, the best we can do is to render the patient physically efficient to stand the severe strain of coughing, which is the worst feature of the disease. Experience has taught us that those children do best who spend their entire time out of doors. We, therefore, advise parents to encourage their children to play in the open air. There is no exception to this rule, even in winter weather, unless it is particularly inclement. If the weather is wet or raw, or if the child has bronchitis, or is running a fever, it would be more safe to keep the child indoors, in a well-aired room, until the temporary conditions pass over, when they could again resume the open-air treatment.

Naturally delicate children if under two years of age should not risk staying out of doors too much in very cold or raw weather, even if not suffering from any of the above complications.

The bedrooms of children suffering from whooping-cough should be large and thoroughly aired day and night.

The nourishment in these cases is of great importance. They should be carefully fed, and if they vomit with the paroxysms of coughing, they should be fed small quantities frequently. Any form of digestive disturbance is very apt to accentuate the frequency of coughing. A fluid diet of milk is the best. Milk punches aid in keeping up the strength; malted milk and eggs beaten in milk are nutritious and easily digested.

So far as internal medication is concerned, I have found pertussin to be the most efficacious remedy. If it is begun early and in sufficient dosage, it not only favors an early termination of the disease, but it lessens the frequency and the severity of the paroxysms. If it is suspected that the child has been exposed to whooping-cough, pertussin may be given during the catarrhal stage with the advantage that it will render the whole course of the disease milder. If it is given during the course of an ordinary catarrhal cold, it will in most cases be as effectual as any ordinary cough remedy. The dosage should be large enough to produce results. I [616] have found a teaspoonful every two hours to a child of three years to be the average dose. In older children I give two teaspoonfuls every three hours. It is necessary to continue its use throughout the disease. The taste of pertussin is pleasant and young children take it willingly.

When the disease is inclined to a protracted course, or when the cough does not subside, especially during unfavorable weather, it is of great importance to send the child away. A change of climate, preferably to the seashore, even for a short time, will act like a charm, and will cure the cough of whooping-cough quicker than any other possible measure.

MEASLES

Measles is the most widely prevalent, eruptive, contagious disease. With few exceptions, every human being "gets" measles. As an uncomplicated disease it is never fatal, and is not even regarded as dangerous. Because of this characteristic, however, parents are neglectful and complications occur, and these frequently prove fatal. One attack renders the patient immune. It is very highly contagious and spreads with great rapidity among those who have never had it. It is not possible to carry the disease any great distance by a third person or by means of living objects. It does not, however, cling to clothing or other objects as long as scarlet fever. Its period of incubation is from eleven to fourteen days.

Symptoms.—The symptoms develop gradually. A severe cold in the head is the first and most characteristic symptom of the disease. There is a discharge from the nose, swollen and watery eyes, sneezing and a hoarse, harsh cough. The patient may complain of the throat being painful and examination will reveal a general congestion of the parts. There are also headache, lassitude, pains in the back, and there may be vomiting and diarrhea. Children in the early stages of measles are tired and sleepy.

Koplik's Spots.—Three or four days, in rare cases somewhat longer, before the appearance of the rash there [617] appears on the mucous membrane of the cheeks small, bluish white, or yellowish white points, the size of a small pin head. These points are surrounded with reddened areas which give the appearance of a general rash with fine white points upon it. These points resemble milk particles. They adhere firmly to the mucous membrane and when an effort is made to remove them it is found that the underlying surface is ulcerated and excoriated.

The Koplik spots are not of much value to the mother other than that they may be relied upon to indicate the coming disease with which they child is affected. Physicians look for them as an aid in diagnosis before the rash would of itself indicate the disease.

The rash appears on the third, fourth, or fifth day of the disease. From the day of the infection to the outbreak of the rash about thirteen days intervene. It is seen first at the roots of the hair on the forehead, behind the ears or on the neck. It may be seen first on the cheeks. The beginning rash appears as small, dark red, dull spots. At first there are only a few, but they soon become more numerous, they join together, and soon the surface looks inflamed as if entirely covered with the rash. The rash covers the entire body, including the soles and palms. In twenty-four hours it is at its height on the face. It spreads downward like a wave, first the face, then the neck and chest, then the abdomen and later the legs. By the time it invades the legs it has begun to fade on the face. It fades slowly in the order of its appearance. Its duration is about four days.

The skin is swollen; it burns and itches. The eyes are swollen and red and intensely sensitive to light. There is usually a mucopus discharge from them. The cough is invariably an annoying feature. The fever is high and reaches its highest point when the rash is at its height. As the rash fades the fever subsides.

When the rash fades, the patient begins to "scale." The scales of measles are fine, like bran, never in large patches like the scales of scarlet fever. The amount of the scaling varies. It may be quite considerable or it may be so small as to be overlooked. [618]

Complications.—The most important and by far the most frequent complication of measles is broncho-pneumonia. There may be various conditions affecting the stomach, bowels, throat, ears, bronchi, and the nervous system, which may accompany the disease but are seldom of a serious or important character.

Treatment.—Measles runs a certain course and will run that course, no matter what we may or may not do. We cannot stop it, or shorten it, or lessen its severity. We can only hope to make the patient comfortable and to prevent the development of complications.

The child should be put in bed and kept comfortably warm but not too warm. The room should be kept at the ordinary temperature of the sick room, 68° to 70° F. It should be darkened but not dark. The food should be fluid and given regularly. The child may be given all the cool,—not cold,—water it wants to drink. The bowels should be kept open daily. If constipation occurs an enema may be given. The eyes must be carefully watched and washed every hour or two during the day with a boracic acid solution. If the cough is distressing, it may be rendered less distressing, though we cannot hope to stop it until the disease has run its course. The restlessness, headache and general discomfort can be much modified by suitable remedies. If the itching is acute, the body can be rubbed with carbolated vaseline. When the rash subsides and the patient is free from fever a daily warm bath should be given in order to facilitate scaling.

Should complications arise they should be promptly cared for by the attending physician.

SUMMARY:—

1. Measles is the most prevalent infectious disease of childhood.

2. The danger of measles has been and is underestimated. Because of its prevalency many mothers treat it with less respect than they should, with the result that fatal complications occur, or the future health of the child is permanently injured. [619]

3. Children with measles should be put in bed and kept in bed and treated as directed above.

The following rules have been formulated by the Department of Health of New York City, with reference to measles, and embody precautions that should find general observance:

1. All children in the family must be promptly excluded from school attendance.

2. Careful and continued isolation of the patient must be enforced until the case is terminated and fumigation has been ordered by the medical inspector of the Department.

3. All secondary cases must be reported even if the first case is still under surveillance of the Department of Health.

4. Suspected cases must be treated as contagious cases until a sufficiently long observation has shown that the patient has a non-contagious disease. All cases will be considered as measles, if so reported. Any change in the original diagnosis must be made in writing to the Department of Health and must be confirmed by a diagnostician.

5. Physicians must not order the removal of patients to the contagious disease hospital, or elsewhere, in cabs or other vehicles, but must notify the Department of Health and the removal will be effected by a coupé or ambulance of the Department.

6. Whenever there is a case of measles in rooms in the rear of, or communicating with, a store, the inspector is required to have the store closed at once, or to report the case for immediate removal to the hospital.

7. A case of measles must not be removed from one house to another, or even to a different apartment in the same house, without the permission of the Department. Such removal is in direct violation of the provisions of the Sanitary Code.

8. No case of measles shall be discharged from observation until the Department has been notified, the case examined by an inspector to see if desquamation is entirely completed, and the premises ordered fumigated. This examination by the inspector is necessary because the Department of Health must have official information as to the completion of desquamation before a child is dismissed from observation. Other people with children demand this protection. At no other time is the inspector allowed to examine the patient. In any case, however, where isolation has not been maintained and it becomes necessary to remove the patient to the hospital, a diagnostician will make an examination.

It is recommended that physicians provide a special washable gown for each case of measles. This gown should be put on before entering the sick-room and taken off outside [620] the sick-room as soon as the visit is completed. The gown should be kept in a closet or suitable place, separate from all other clothing, and the gown, and the closet should be fumigated after the termination of the case.

10. In private houses only fumigation may be performed under the supervision of the attending physician; provided he follow accurately the directions given in the following rules and regulations. Upon request a blank will be provided upon which he must state the manner and extent of the work performed under his orders and supervision. If satisfactory to the Department, this will be accepted in place of fumigation by the Department. It is

essential, however, that he should know that the disinfection has been efficiently carried out.

In every case of fumigation the following regulations must be complied with:

All cracks or crevices in rooms to be fumigated must be sealed or calked, to prevent the escape of the disinfectant, and one of the following disinfectants used in the quantities named:

a. Sulphur, 4 lbs., for every 1,000 cubic feet of air space, 8 hours' exposure.

b. Formaline, 6 oz. for every 1,000 cubic feet of air space, 4 hours' exposure.

c. Paraform, 1,000 grains for every 1,000 cubic feet of air space, 6 hours' exposure.

The following disinfecting solutions may be used for goods, which are afterwards to be washed:

a. Carbolic acid, 2 to 5 per cent.

b. Bichloride of mercury, 1-1,000.

SCARLET FEVER. SCARLATINA.

Scarlet fever is an acute, contagious disease. It begins abruptly. The child may have a severe attack and be quite sick from the beginning, or he may have a mild attack and not be very sick. Usually the fever rises rapidly, the child vomits and complains of a sore throat. If the attack is very mild the throat symptoms may not cause any distress. Frequently, about the third day, there are patches on the tonsils. Prostration may be profound if the fever is very high. Convulsions and diarrhea are sometimes present in very young patients. It takes from two to six days to develop scarlet fever from the time the child is exposed to it. The disease may be caught at any time, but it is most contagious [621] during the time the patient is scaling. It is not as contagious as measles. Some children seem to escape even though directly exposed to it. It is more frequent in the fall and during the winter, and it is more severe during the latter months.

Eruption.—The eruption appears at any time after twelve hours. It may not, however, appear before the third or fourth day. It lasts from three to seven days, and only takes a few hours to cover the whole body after it is first seen. The rash is first seen on the neck or chest; it appears as a red, uniform blush, but, when examined closely, small reddish spots may be seen all over it. If the rash is very faint and of a doubtful character a hot bath may bring it out. A bright red, well-developed rash is a sign of good heart action. In the event of heart failure, the rash fades quickly. Itching is a constant symptom after the rash is fully out.

About the eighth day the rash begins to scale or desquamate. It begins on the neck and chest. It takes from one to three weeks to scale completely, from the time it begins to peel. The hands and feet are the last spots to scale.

It must always be kept in mind that mild cases are just as contagious as severe cases, and that a mild case may cause in another person a very severe attack.

The throat may be mildly affected or it may be the most troublesome feature of the case. It is red and swollen and the child complains of pain during the act of swallowing. Patches may be seen on the tonsils on the third day. There is usually a discharge from the nose and this discharge may be contagious. While the fever is high, the child is restless, complains of thirst, and may be slightly delirious.

One attack is usually all a child has during life, though there are exceptions to this rule. Complications are quite frequent with scarlet fever. Inflammation of the ears and kidneys is most often met.

Measures to be Taken to Prevent Spread of Disease.—Every case, no matter how mild, should be isolated for four weeks. Many cases must be isolated longer,—until scaling is complete. Children should not play or [622] sleep with other children for three or four weeks after all symptoms have been absent. Other children in the family, who have not been exposed, should be sent away. All clothing should be changed and washed in soap and water and then boiled in a carbolic solution. The nurse should not mix freely with other members of the family. The sick room should be kept clean, and well aired. It should be dusted with a wet cloth, and this should afterwards be burned. There should be no furniture, or hangings, or pictures in the room other than are absolutely necessary. The room should not be used after the case is over until it is thoroughly and completely disinfected.

During the period of scaling the patient should be rubbed all over with carbolated vaseline. This allays itching and prevents the scales flying around. The bed sheet can be taken off daily with the scales in it, and immediately put in carbolic water and boiled.

Treatment.—Inasmuch as scarlet fever is one of the most dangerous and one of the most treacherous diseases of childhood, we cannot afford to take any chances with it. Every child with scarlet fever should be put in bed, and kept there during the entire illness,—that is, from four to six weeks. Light, and the free circulation of fresh air are absolutely necessary for the proper care of a scarlet fever case. The child should be clothed only with the usual night gown and a light undershirt. No extra wraps or blankets are required.

The diet should be reduced in quantity and strength. The bowels should move daily. If anything is necessary to accomplish this, citrate of magnesia is quite satisfactory. There is no special medicine for the treatment of this disease. Often it is not necessary to give any. Good nursing is more essential, and with proper attention to the bowels, diet, fresh air, clothing, sleep, and quiet, all will, as a rule, result favorably. Quiet is essential. Consequently, two persons at a time should never be allowed in the room with the little patient.

The family physician will prescribe whatever medicine is necessary in his judgment, and will meet any complication as it arises. [623]

TYPHOID FEVER

Typhoid fever is an acute infectious disease. It is rare in infancy. After the fifth year it is more common. It is caused by drinking infected water or milk. It is not a serious disease in childhood, rarely being fatal.

Symptoms.—It may begin suddenly or it may come on slowly. If suddenly, the child develops what appears to be an attack of indigestion, has fever, vomiting, and is prostrated. In cases developing slowly the child complains of being tired, has a headache, nausea, and fever. Vomiting is the suggestive and important symptom.

Diarrhea is usually present. Constipation, however, may accompany the entire illness. Children may not complain of an excess of gas as do adults. The abdomen is tender. The typhoid eruption is rarely seen in children. They lose flesh steadily and then strength diminishes rapidly. Headache and delirium at night are quite common, and the child is dull and indifferent, and often in a state of semi-stupor.

In order to tell definitely whether the child has typhoid, it is necessary to make a blood examination. There are so many intestinal conditions in children that simulate typhoid, that a blood examination is imperative.

Treatment.—The patient should remain in bed during the time fever is present and for a few days after. A fluid diet, preferably milk, is the most suitable means of nourishing the child. It may be diluted or given plain according to the age of the patient. Water is essential and should be given freely.

The discharges of the patient should be thoroughly disinfected in a solution of carbolic acid, 1-20. All clothing and bed linen should be boiled for two hours. If the fever remains high cold sponging is advisable. The attending physician should instruct regarding this feature, as some children do not stand cold applications well.

The average duration of the disease is about six weeks.

How to Keep From Getting and Spreading Typhoid Fever.—Typhoid fever is a communicable disease, but, if certain precautions are taken, its contraction and spread can almost certainly be prevented. [624]

The disease is caused by a specific germ known as the typhoid bacillus. These germs are found in the excreta (stools and urine) of persons ill with typhoid fever.

Failure to properly disinfect these excreta and carelessness in the care of persons ill with typhoid fever lead to the transmission of the disease from the sick to the well by the infection of water, milk or food with the typhoid bacillus or by direct contact.

The disease is contracted by taking into the mouth in some form the discharges from some previous case. There is no other way. It is, therefore, a disease of filth and someone is at fault somewhere for every case of typhoid fever that occurs.

Bad sanitary conditions, such as lack of drainage, open cesspools, sewer gas, decaying vegetable matter, etc., may favor the contraction of the disease, but cannot cause it unless the specific germ, the typhoid bacillus, is present.

The water supply of a community becomes infected by the entrance into it of the excreta (stools and urine) of persons suffering from typhoid fever.

Milk (in which typhoid bacilli grow and multiply very rapidly) usually becomes infected by washing out milk cans with water in which these bacilli are present, or from the presence of the bacilli on the hands or persons of those handling milk. Oysters spread the disease when they have been "freshed" in water rich in sewage and containing the typhoid bacillus. Flies, whose bodies have become foul with typhoid excreta, may infect food, milk, etc. Those who take care of typhoid patients may contract the disease if they do not at once disinfect their hands after handling the patient, or clothing or bedding which has become soiled with the discharges.

How to Keep From Getting Typhoid Fever.—If the chance of infection is to be reduced to a minimum, all drinking water, concerning the character of which there may be the slightest doubt, should be boiled, and all milk, the handling and care of which is not absolutely beyond suspicion, should be pasteurized or boiled. All food supplies (meat, milk, vegetables, etc.), should be carefully [625] protected against flies, and flies should not be permitted access to the sick-room, the kitchen nor to the room in which the meals are eaten. Bathing at all beaches which have sewers emptying in their immediate vicinity should be strictly avoided. In the majority of cases it is probable that the system must be slightly below par in order that the disease may be contracted; therefore, all indigestible food, green fruit, etc., which may set up indigestion or diarrhea, and so render the system more susceptible to infection, should be avoided. In addition, the elementary rules of cleanliness and hygiene, both as to the house and person, should be most strictly observed. No member of a household in which a case of typhoid fever occurs should take food in any form without previously washing the hands.

Typhoid bacilli enter the body only through the mouth. If sufficient care be taken to prevent their entrance, the contraction of the disease can be absolutely prevented.

How to Keep From Spreading the Disease.—In order to protect themselves and others in the household, persons caring for or in any way coming into contact with a case of typhoid fever must constantly bear in mind that the secretions and excretions (urine, stools, etc.), of the patient contain typhoid bacilli and are capable of transmitting the disease to others. The person who nurses the patient should not do the cooking for the family. The bedding used by the patient should be washed separately from that used by others. Special dishes, plates, knives, forks, etc., should be kept for the use of the patient alone, and should be washed separately and thoroughly. Particular attention should be paid to immediate disinfection of the stools and urine of the patients until the restoration of health is complete.

The urine is especially dangerous. It may look entirely normal and yet contain typhoid bacilli for some time after recovery is apparently complete. In a few instances the typhoid bacilli may persist in the stools for weeks or months after recovery. Such persons are called "typhoid carriers," and constitute a grave menace to the health of the community. The best disinfectants are carbolic acid and freshly slacked lime; both are effectual, [626] cheap and easily obtained. Urine or stools to which has been added one-third of their volume of a solution of one part of carbolic acid to twenty parts of water are, as a rule, sufficiently disinfected in half an hour, provided the mass of the stool is broken up and thoroughly mixed with the solutions. The best method is to keep the urinal of bed-pan partly filled with the disinfecting solution at all times. In this way any germs present in the urine or stools are almost instantly destroyed. Stools and urine should never be thrown out on the ground. If no system of drainage is at hand, they should be very thoroughly disinfected and emptied into a hole in the ground and covered with earth. All persons nursing or handling the patient in any way should be careful to wash their hands very thoroughly with soap and water before leaving the sick-room. They should never, while in the sick-room, touch any article of food or put their hands to their mouths. Careful observation of the above suggestions and precautions will almost certainly prevent contraction of typhoid fever or the spread of the disease.

VARIOUS SOLUTIONS

Boracic Acid Solution.—In the previous pages mothers are frequently told to use "a saturated solution of boracic acid." A saturated solution means that the water in the solution has dissolved all of the product that is put into it that it is capable of dissolving. When boracic acid is put into water, the water will dissolve it up to a certain point; if you add more the boracic acid will not dissolve; it will float if it is in the form of powder, or it will remain at the bottom of the glass if it is crystal—in other words the water is saturated to its limit and the solution is known as a saturated solution.

The strength of a saturated solution of boracic acid is as follows:—

Boracic Acid   Ounces   1-1/2

Hot Sterile Water Pints   2

which means that 2 pints of hot water will completely dissolve 1-1/2 ounces of boracic acid. If any more boracic [627] acid is added the water will not dissolve it because it is already "saturated." Inasmuch, however, as boracic acid is harmless, it is perfectly safe to use the liquid part of a solution which contains some undissolved acid.

A saturated solution is used in the eyes after it is strained.

Normal Salt Solution.—A normal salt solution is made in the following proportions:—

Sodium Chloride (ordinary table salt) Grains 128

Sterile Water   Pints   2

Normal salt solution is much used in irrigating the bowel. A mother may safely use it in the proportion of one heaping teaspoonful to two quarts of water—two quarts being the size of the ordinary fountain syringe.

Carron Oil.—Lime water and raw linseed oil, equal parts. This mixture is much used in burns. It should be made fresh.

Thiersch's Solution:—

Salicylic Acid   Drams   1/2

Boracic Acid   Drams   3

Sterile Water   Pints   2

Thiersch's solution is a good, mild antiseptic solution, or wash.

Solution of Bichloride of Mercury (1 to 1000):—

Bichloride of Mercury   Grains   15

Common Salt   Grains   15

Sterile Water   Pints   2

Bichloride of mercury is one of the most powerful and poisonous drugs. Solutions made from it should never be used without special directions from a physician. In much weaker solutions than the above it is one of the best antiseptic washes known. It is used to disinfect wounds, for douches, and for various other purposes, but always by special direction of a physician.

Other solutions.—Frequently mothers are directed to use solutions in the proportion of 1 to 500, or 1 to 1000.

This means that there will be one part of the drug, or of [628] the liquid medicine, to 500, or 1000 parts of water. For example if you were asked to make up a solution of bichloride of mercury in the strength of 1 to 4000, you would use one ounce of bichloride of mercury to four thousand ounces of water, or one grain of the mercury to four thousand drops of water,—one grain being equivalent to one drop.

Sometimes solutions are made up on the percentage basis. For example, a five per cent. solution of carbolic acid. In this case it would be necessary to take five ounces of carbolic to one hundred ounces of water, or five drops of carbolic to one hundred drops of water.

[629]
CHAPTER XXXIX

ACCIDENTS AND EMERGENCIES

Accidents and Emergencies—Contents of the Family Medicine Chest—Foreign Bodies in the Eye—Foreign Bodies in the Ear—Foreign Bodies in the Nose—Foreign Bodies in the Throat—A Bruise or Contusion—Wounds—Arrest of Hemorrhage—Removal of Foreign Bodies from a Wound—Cleansing a Wound—Closing and Dressing Wounds—The Condition of Shock—Dog Bites—Sprains— Dislocations—Wounds of the Scalp—Run-around—Felon—Whitlow—Burns and Scalds

Contents of the Family Medicine Chest.—The family medicine cabinet should contain the following articles: a graduate, medicine droppers, hot water bags, a flat ice bag, a fountain syringe, a Davidson's syringe, a baby syringe, sterile gauze, absorbent cotton, gauze bandages of various widths, a yard of oiled silk, one roll of one inch "Z O" adhesive plaster, a bottle of Pearson's creolin, hydrogen peroxide (fresh), one ounce tincture of iodine in an air-tight bottle, a can of Colman's mustard, two ounces of syrup of ipecac, a bottle of castor oil (fresh), one pound of boracic acid powder, one pound of boracic acid crystal, a bottle of glycerine, a bottle of white vaseline, a bath thermometer, some good whisky or brandy, aromatic spirits of ammonia, smelling salts, pure sodium bicarbonate, oil of cloves for an aching gum or toothache, a bottle of alkolol for mouth wash and gargle, and one ounce of the following ointment for use in the various emergencies which occur in all homes,—

Bismuth subnitrate   dram one

Zinc oxide   dram one

Phenol (95%)   drops twelve

Resinol ointment to make ounce one

This ointment may be applied to all cuts, bruises, skin eruptions, chafings and sores of minor importance. It is one of the best applications for chafing of the skin in babies. [630]

The medicine chest should also contain a small jar of Unguentine for burns; one-tenth grain calomel tablets for a cathartic for baby to be used as explained in the text of the book, or as advised by the physician. It may also contain tablets for colds and for other purposes as suggested by the family physician. It should never contain medicines the use of which is not thoroughly understood by the mother. It is a wrong practice for mothers to keep medicines to use for the same ailment at a subsequent time. The ailment may not be the same and frequently the medicine itself deteriorates, or it may get stronger with age. Many medicines are made with alcohol in them. If kept for some time the alcohol evaporates and leaves a concentrated mixture which, if given in the dose meant for the fresh preparation, may poison a child. Such cases of poisoning are on record. The same argument applies to powders. Certain drugs lose their strength, some absorb moisture, others change their chemical strength if kept mixed with other chemicals. They should be thrown away after the case is over if they have not been used. It is a dangerous practice to keep medicines around if there are children in the family.

Foreign Bodies in the Eye.—Particles which accidentally lodge in the eye are usually located on the under surface of the upper lid. They are sometimes, however, found on the ball of the eye or on the inner aspect of the lower lid. Foreign bodies which are propelled into the eye with great force, as iron specks which railroad men frequently get sometimes imbed themselves into the eye-ball and have to be cut out or dug out. The entrance of the foreign particle is always accompanied by a flow of tears which is nature's way of removing them. The offending object may escape through the tear duct into the nose, or it may be simply washed out with the flow of tears. Rubbing the well eye will cause a flow of tears in both eyes and may facilitate removal of the foreign matter. Blowing the nose may force the particle into the tear duct. The use of the eye cup may help in ridding the eye of the body. The same object may be accomplished if the eyes are immersed in a basin of water and opened wide. Then by moving the eyes [631] around the particle may be washed out. If the particle is located on the under surface of the upper lid it may be promptly removed by pulling the upper lid forcibly down and over the lower lid. The eyelashes of the lower lid act as a brush and as a rule quickly remove the irritant if the procedure is carried out adroitly. Everting the upper lid is a means of locating the body and in making possible its removal by a small camel's hair brush or corner of a handkerchief. To evert the upper lid it is necessary to employ a guide. A match stem may be used in an emergency. This is laid across the middle of the upper lid, the eye lashes are grasped with the fingers of the other hand and the lid is bent over the match stem and turned up thus everting or turning inside out the entire upper lid. The procedure may be facilitated if the patient is instructed to look down while the operator is drawing the eye-lid upward.

If the particle cannot be easily removed by any of the above methods it is not safe for an uninstructed individual to go any further. The eye is an exceedingly delicate organ and may be permanently injured by unnecessary irritation. It is always safer and it may be cheaper in the long run to consult a competent oculist in such cases.

After the removal of any object from the eye, it is desirable to frequently wash it out with a saturated solution of boracic acid. This mixture will allay any inflammation and will tend to restore the normal condition more quickly and more satisfactorily than if the eye were left to heal itself.

Foreign Bodies in the Ear.—When a foreign body gets into the ear mothers are unnecessarily alarmed because of a failure to appreciate that the ear is a closed passage. It is impossible for any object to get into the ear itself; the depth of the external passage is only about one inch in an adult. At this point the passage is completely closed by the drum membrane. Most of the harm is done by ignorant meddling, not by the object itself.

Children frequently put foreign bodies in the ear, as, buttons, pebbles, beans, cherry stones, coffee, etc. The very first thing for the mother to do when she learns that her child has put "something" in its ear is to keep cool, [632] and try to find out what the something is. It is essential to know what the article is because different articles are treated differently. For example if we try to remove a bean or pea with a syringe, the liquid will cause the pea or bean to swell and result in wedging it in so firmly that it will be impossible to dislodge it in this way.

If the object is hard, as a marble, button, pebble, bead, the greatest care must be exercised. Try to make the object fall out. To effect this, turn the child's head downward with the injured ear toward the floor. Then pull the lobe of the ear outward and backward so as to straighten the canal. A teaspoonful of olive oil poured into the ear will aid in its expulsion. If after the oil is poured in, the head is suddenly turned as above described the object will fall out. A very effective way to remove a hard object is to take a small camel's hair brush and coat the end with glue, or any other adhesive substance, then place it in contact with the object and permit it to remain long enough to become firmly attached after which it may be gently pulled out with the object attached. Never employ an instrument in the ear to remove a foreign body.

When a live insect or fly enters the ear a number of safe methods may be developed. If the ear is immediately turned to a bright light the insect may come out of its own accord. It may be floated out with salt water, or it may be smothered with sweet oil or castor oil after which it may be floated or syringed out. If it is necessary to employ a syringe this should be used gently. A foreign body may remain in the ear for days or weeks without doing any harm. This suggests that any unnecessary poking or prying should not be undertaken, because this may wedge it in tighter and to injure the drum membrane.

Foreign Bodies in the Nose.—Children may put any of these articles into the nose. Very often they do, and do not know enough to tell. If such is the case the first symptom calling attention to the fact that something is wrong is the appearance of a thick foul discharge from one nostril or some obstruction to breathing on the same side. [633]

When the foreign body may be seen the child should be made to blow the nose, first closing the well side with the finger. If this does not expel the object the child should be made to sneeze by tickling the free nostril with a feather or by taking snuff. The mother should never permit the use of instruments by one unskilled in an effort to rid the nose of an obstruction. There is great danger of seriously injuring the delicate structure of the nose in this way or of pushing the object so far in that it may necessitate an operation to extract it. It is much safer to seek medical aid before any damage is effected. It seldom does harm to wait until the right assistance is at hand; it often does serious harm to be too smart in these little matters.

Foreign Bodies in the Throat.—If the foreign body is in the upper part of the throat and can be seen it may be removed with any instrument that can grasp it. The child may be immediately held up by its feet when the article may be shaken out. If it is further back or in the air passages the child should be made to vomit by tickling the throat with a feather or with the finger held in the throat till it does vomit.

When the object interferes with breathing a physician should be sent for in a hurry. In the meantime the family may try to dislodge it by having the child bend forward or by holding it with the head downward and, while in this position, sharply striking the back with each cough. Striking the chest when in this position may effect the same purpose. If no success follows this procedure try the reverse position. Have the child bend backward over the arm of a sofa, for example, or put him in bed with the body hanging out of the bed face upward. If none of these effect relief you must depend upon the skill of the physician.

A Bruise or Contusion.—A bruise or contusion is an injury to the tissues underneath the skin, but this does not imply that the skin itself is opened or damaged. In every bruise the small blood vessels are ruptured, and the blood collects in the tissues causing distention, swelling and pain. The blood is held in the tissues, it is stagnant, becomes dark in color and so produces the bluish [634] discoloration that we see in all bruises. The color varies according to the extent of the collected blood. At first it is red and inflamed looking, then purple, then black, then greenish and finally citron. The so-called "black-eye" is a typical example of this degree of bruise. After a bruise the parts swell from the collection of blood and from the accompanying inflammation. This causes pain which persists for a day although the spot may be sore and tender for a week or more.

In all mild varieties home remedies may suffice, but in the more serious and extensive bruises it is advisable to seek medical assistance. It is essential to completely put the part to rest and to elevate it. This will relieve the pain and favor the absorption of the exuded blood. If the bruise is on the foot, the leg should be elevated until the foot is higher than the hip. If, on the hand, it should be so held that it will be higher than the elbow and it may frequently be held higher than the shoulder to relieve the throbbing and the pain.

As a rule, cold should be applied as soon after the injury as possible, cloths wrung out of ice water, or a piece of ice may be bound on the part for a short time. The object of the cold is to stop the internal bleeding. If the injury is slight, as are most of the injuries of the household, the mother may apply repeated cloths wrung out of very hot water. This procedure tends to aid the immediate absorption of the blood and prevents a discoloration of the part. If there is great pain relief may be afforded by applying a firm bandage saturated in the lead-water and laudanum mixture which may be obtained in the drug store under the name of lead and opium wash. The bruised part should be massaged every day and a simple ointment may be applied to soften the inflamed area.

If any complication arises in the treatment of a bruise, it will be necessary to consult a physician.

Wounds.—A wound implies an injury to the skin in addition to injury to the underlying parts to a lesser or greater extent. The skin may be opened by cutting, or stabbing wounds; or it may be punctured, torn, contused, or bruised open. These injuries are effected in [635] various ways. We speak of machinery or mechanical wounds, or gunshot wounds, bites, cuts, stabs and other varieties of wounds.

It is very important to know exactly how a wound is produced and the nature of the instrument which opened the skin. We try to obtain this information in order to estimate the probable degree of poison that may or may not have entered into the wound.

The first thing to do in treating wounds is to stop the bleeding. If the patient is suffering from shock he should be given active treatment for this condition as described elsewhere. If the wound contains any foreign bodies these should be removed. The wound should then be cleansed, closed and dressed and kept at rest. If the wound is poisoned, or if there is any fear that lockjaw may arise, or if the wound has been caused by a mad dog it will require special treatment.

It is far better not to interfere if you do not know what to do than to do harm. One should offer no advice if they are not qualified to give advice. Much harm has resulted from doing the wrong thing in these cases. The instruction in the following pages is given so that the average mother may know what to do in emergency but not with the intention that she may regard her knowledge as sufficient to dispense with the aid of the physician.

Arrest of Hemorrhage.—When there is a wound there is always bleeding; this means that some blood vessels have been cut or torn open allowing blood to escape. The character of the hemorrhage will determine the nature of the treatment to be employed. On general principles, the first thing to do in the presence of bleeding is to elevate the part, if that is possible. If there is simply a general oozing of blood, it may be controlled and arrested by pressure. This pressure should be steady and prolonged. It is best accomplished by wetting a clean handkerchief or a pad of gauze in ice cold water, placing this on the part and binding it on firmly with a bandage.

If the discharge of blood flows in a steady stream and is rather dark the hemorrhage is coming from a vein. [636] We know that veins carry blood toward the heart so that any pressure or constriction employed to stop a venous hemorrhage should be tied on the side of the wound further removed from the heart. Inasmuch as veins have soft walls the right kind of pressure will in most instances stop the bleeding. The part should be elevated after the pad is adjusted in place. Any tight band on the limb as a garter or sleeve band should be removed as they tend to interrupt the return circulation.

If the hemorrhage is from an artery the blood is bright red. It spurts out forcibly, is difficult to control and demands immediate attention. Arteries carry the blood from the heart to the extremities. They beat with every pulsation of the heart so that blood coming from an artery spurts with every pulse beat. Even a small artery may be responsible for a very considerable hemorrhage in a very short time. Whatever is done must be done quickly. The parts should be freed from all clothing and if possible elevated. Pressure may be tried, if it succeeds it must be strong and steady pressure. The point to press must be on the heart side of the bleeding artery since the blood stream is coming that way—this the mother will note is the reverse from treating bleeding from a vein as previously explained. The artery at this point may be felt beating. It is frequently necessary to clamp the whole limb to stop an arterial hemorrhage. This may be done in the following manner. Take a strong piece of cloth or bandage and tie above the bleeding point. Insert a short piece of stick between the bandage and the limb and twist around until the bleeding stops. This should not be kept on longer than one hour. A tourniquet of this character shuts off all the blood in the limb and if kept on too long the parts may mortify. The best means to stop a hemorrhage of this character is by means of a rubber bandage sold for the purpose. It is applied by stretching at every turn. It exerts uniform pressure and in this way does no injury to the parts. All these measures are, of course, only temporary expedients as the artery will finally have to be caught and tied by a physician.

Removal of Foreign Bodies From a Wound.—When [637] the foreign bodies are large enough to be seen they may be picked out with the fingers after the hands have been rendered sterile. Smaller bodies may be picked up with forceps, or they may be washed out with water that has been boiled and cooled slightly, or a bichloride of mercury solution in the strength of 1 to 2000 may be used; or a normal salt solution may be used. As a general rule the physician should be allowed to undertake this procedure so that you may not be blamed for something that may come up later.

Cleansing a Wound.—The simplest way, and the most effective, to cleanse a wound, no matter how caused, is to procure a brush and paint it thoroughly with tincture of iodine. The iodine should be painted right into the raw wound, it is then bound up and left if it is small and does not need any stitching. When the physician comes he can attend to any further procedure that may be necessary.

Closing and Dressing Wounds.—If the wound is small, its edges may be drawn together with narrow strips of adhesive bandage after it has been painted with iodine. It is then bound up and kept at rest. It should be inspected the following day to see if it is healing properly.

If the wound is large or torn, it should be seen by a physician and dressed and closed by him. All wounds do better if they are kept at rest.

The Condition of Shock.—When a person suffers a serious injury, loses a large quantity of blood, or is subjected to a profound emotion, it affects the vital powers to such an extent that the individual is said to be suffering from shock. Shock expresses itself in varying degrees of apathy. The patient may or may not be conscious. If conscious he gives no evidence of feeling, he is silent and motionless although he will respond to directions and may answer questions. The eyes are dull and listless, the face pale and pinched, and the general expression is apathetic. The skin is cold and there may be perspiration; the pulse is feeble and irregular, and the breathing is shallow. The whole attitude of the victim is one of indifference and apparent inability to [638] appreciate the seriousness of the situation and a seeming immunity to pain or discomfort.

When this condition exists it must always be regarded as serious because the patient may die as a direct result of the condition of shock. The various symptoms depend upon a temporary paralysis of the blood vessels which deprives the brain of blood. There is always a certain degree of shock with all injuries. Mothers should know what to do in these cases before the physician comes. The general treatment in all cases is to keep the patient warm and quiet, and to use stimulants carefully.

The patient should be put in bed or on a flat surface with the feet higher than the head. If raising the feet should cause the face to become blue it will be advisable to restore the patient to the horizontal posture. Artificial heat must be applied to the patient's body and extremities by means of hot water bags, bottles, bricks, plates, or any other handy device. Blankets should be put around the patient and every possible means resorted to, to maintain body heat. Mustard plasters may be put to the heart, spine and shins. Stimulants are necessary, such as hot black coffee if possible or hot water, in which a small portion of brandy may be put. If brandy is not obtainable the patient may take aromatic spirits of ammonia in hot water every twenty minutes for a number of doses. In every case of shock a physician should be sent for immediately.

Dog Bites.—When a child is bit by a dog every effort should be made to get the dog. It should be kept in a safe place for a week so that it may be definitely known whether it is sick or not. If the dog dies within a few days after biting anyone it may be assumed that he had rabies. Its head should be sent to the local health authorities who can tell after examination if it was mad. If there is any reason to assume that the dog was infected, the child should receive the Pasteur treatment. This treatment will, if conducted under favorable circumstances, absolutely prevent hydrophobia.

The mother should sterilize the wound as thoroughly as possible. This may be done by using pure hydrogen peroxide. A little piece of absorbent cotton is wound [639] round the end of a tooth-pick or match, dipped in the peroxide and the incision thoroughly rubbed clean. This may be done a number of times to ensure thorough cleansing. No effort should be made to cauterize the wound. It is not considered proper to employ this method with dog bites. When the physician examines the wound he may or may not open it further for more extensive inspection and sterilization.

Mothers should remember that there are thousands of bites by dogs that never cause any trouble, and if it is known that the dog is healthy no worry need trouble the family. It is also wrong to inform the child of the probability of hydrophobia. The child may worry himself sick with fear and if the mother is nervous and excitable he is apt to be made sick with the dread of what may follow. It is better, therefore, to remain quiet, to keep cool, and not to excite the little patient at all.

Sprains.—Every joint is held together by ligaments which are attached to the bones forming the joint. If these ligaments are subjected to a sudden twist in a direction in which the joint is not constructed to move, the resulting injury is known as a sprain. The ligaments are stretched, though they may be torn apart and even small pieces of the bone may be split off if the wrench is great enough. The injury is an exceedingly painful one and frequently renders the limb useless for some time. It is always accompanied with some degree of swelling and more or less inflammation.

A sprained joint should be immediately put at absolute rest. The best dressing is the lead and opium wash. Two pints of it may be obtained at the drug store. Pour into a large bowl, saturate a large piece of thick absorbent cotton, wrap around the joint and bind in place. This dressing may be repeated as often as the cotton becomes dry. When the swelling has disappeared and the pain is gone, it is desirable to have the joint supported with strips of adhesive bandage. These must be put on in a certain way in order to properly support the joint. Consequently a physician should put them on. If a sprain is not attended to effectively there is danger of the joint being more or less incapacitated for life. [640]

Dislocations.—A dislocated joint is one that has been put out of place. It is best to allow a physician to treat a dislocation. Unskilled handling of a dislocated joint may not only increase the damage but it may permanently put the joint out of business. Until the physician arrives the part should be kept absolutely at rest.

Wounds of the Scalp.—Children frequently get injuries of the scalp. These wounds bleed freely and as a rule they occasion a great deal of unnecessary worry and apprehension. Usually they are not of much importance. We must keep in mind, however, the probability of fracture as a consequence of severe injury. The first thing to do when there is bleeding from the scalp is to cut or shave away the hair surrounding the wound. This should be done for an inch around the wound so that thorough disinfection may be possible. The wound should now be cleansed as previously instructed and an effort made to stop the bleeding. The best method is to first apply pads of gauze wrung out of very hot water. When success is evident a pad made of boiled cotton should be placed on the wound and held tightly in place for some time. If the wound is of such a character as to demand stitches a physician should of course put them in.

Run-Around: Felon: Whitlow.—When pus germs enter around a finger nail and lodge in the soft tissue a "run-around" is the result. It is accompanied with pain, swelling, redness and inflammation. The loss of the nail may follow.

A felon or Whitlow is a more extensive and a more serious condition. It is not always possible to trace the cause of a felon. The fact that germs gain an entrance, however, is soon established. Sometimes a bruise, or scratch, or a wound is the primary cause. The last joint of any of the fingers may be the seat of a felon. A end of the finger becomes hot, tense, swollen and very painful; the pain is intense if the hand is held down. The surface may or may not be red. There is as a rule some fever. If the felon is on the little finger or thumb the condition is worse than on the others as a rule,—the inflammation extending to the hand and often into the arm. [641] The condition affects the palmar surface of the fingers. If the felon results in the "death" of the bone, the last joint will have to be taken off and the hand may be distorted, crippled, and rendered permanently disabled. Blood poison may set in and death is possible as a result of this complication.

Treatment.—Every effort should be made to abort a felon. Continuous application of equal parts of alcohol and water night and day may abort it. Tincture of iodine applied to the entire end of the finger may be effective. The hand must be at rest, carried in a sling during the day and slung over the head to the bedboard at night. If these efforts are not successful after twenty-four hours hot poultices should be resorted to, but they must be changed every twenty minutes. If, at the end of another twenty-four hours, there is no improvement the finger must be freely cut open by a surgeon and the poultices continued.

Treatment of "Run-Around."—Apply iodine freely, cold applications, and if the inflammation persists use poultices. It is frequently necessary to incise the run-around. Patients suffering from either of these conditions need general tonic treatment and should be under the care of a physician.

Burns and Scalds.—Burns result from undue exposure to dry heat. Scalds are produced by the action of hot liquids and steam.

There are always produced two results from a burn or a scald. First the local effect, and, second, the general effect. The general effect may produce shock, the symptoms of which have been described in the previous pages. The degree of shock depends upon the extent of the local injury and may be severe enough to result in death. If the local injury covers more than two-thirds of the body death as a rule takes place within two days.

How to Extinguish Burning Clothing.—The thought to keep in mind is to smother the flames effectively. If we deprive the flame of all air or oxygen it will immediately subside. This may be done quickly by wrapping the burning part in a carpet, rug, blanket, overcoat or any large woolen material at hand. If none of these [642] articles are at hand the victim may roll on the floor and try to smother the flame by pressure, aided by the hands. It is a good plan to throw water on the patient immediately after the fire has been put out, so as to extinguish the smoldering fire.

When a person is scalded by steam or boiling water or other liquid, it is advisable to pour cold water freely over the wound.

How to Remove the Clothing.—When it is necessary to remove the clothing it is essential to be gentle in order not to do greater injury. The clothing must not be pulled. The garment should be cut so that they fall off. If any part sticks to the skin, it must be left, not torn away. Later, it may be removed by moistening it with salt water.

Treatment of Scalds and Burns.—All slight burns or scalds may be effectively treated with Unguentine. This substance may be obtained in any drug store. It is spread on a cloth and applied directly to the injured part, bound securely on and renewed every day until the wound is healed. If Unguentine is not readily obtainable the part may be covered with any of the following mixtures or oils: carbolated vaseline, equal parts of linseed oil and lime water, olive oil, castor oil or kerosene, cloths soaked in a solution of baking soda, or a solution of phenol sodique.

In severe burns or scalds the mother should not attempt to treat the child. A physician should be summoned at once. The child may be given a little whisky or brandy in warm water, and if the pain is great a dose of laudanum may be given. The dose of laudanum is one drop for each year of life. If the child has a chill he may be put into a warm bath of 100°F. It is not wise to cut a burn blister. The water may be let out by puncturing with a sterile needle, but the skin must be left intact until the new skin is grown. The treatment of burns must be done with the greatest cleanliness because if infected with germs they may prove serious.

[643]

MISCELLANEOUS

[644]

[645]

CHAPTER XL

MISCELLANEOUS

The Dangerous House Fly—Diseases Transmitted by Flies—Homes Should be Carefully Screened and Protected—The Breeding Places of Flies—Special Care Should be Given to Stables, Privy Vaults, Garbage, Vacant Lots, Foodstuffs, Water Fronts, Drains—Precautions to be Observed—How to Kill Flies—Moths—What Physicians are Doing—Radium—X-Ray Treatment and X-Ray Diagnosis—Aseptic Surgery—New Anesthetics—Vaccine in Typhoid Fever—"606"—Transplanting the Organs of Dead Men into the Living—Bacteria that Make Soil Barren or Productive—Anti-meningitis Serum—A Serum for Malaria in Sight.

THE DANGEROUS HOUSE FLY

Mothers should become thoroughly acquainted with the grave consequences which may result from fly-infected foods, and from the possible carriage of disease by means of flies, even where foods are carefully protected. The transmission of the following diseases by means of flies has been conclusively proven: typhoid fever, tuberculosis, cholera, Oriental plague, inflammation of the eyelids, serious infection of wounds. Summer diarrhea of children is also transmitted in this way.

Typhoid fever and summer diarrhea of children in this country, and cholera and Oriental plague in the countries in which those diseases exist, may be transmitted through the various foods that are eaten in an uncooked state, if infected by flies, through cooked foods infected by flies after the process of cooking, through drinking water which has been infected by flies, and through milk similarly infected. Fruits are especially likely to be infected by the small fruit fly commonly found around markets and stands. Fish may be infected by flies, and in consequence will undergo rapid decomposition. Decomposition caused in this way has [646] resulted in many cases of diarrhea and dysentery. What is commonly known as fly speck is the excreta of the fly, and frequently contains virulent disease germs. These specks are often found on foodstuffs that have not been properly protected.

Transmission of disease may also occur by the infection of open wounds through contact with infected flies. This is true of all pus formation in wounds. The simple contact of a fly infected with the disease may cause Oriental plague, sore eyes, and possibly granular eyelids. A fly infected with dysentery or typhoid fever may cause either of these diseases by simply coming in contact with the lips of susceptible persons.

The fly in the house should be relentlessly pursued and destroyed. The house which is carefully screened and protected from flies is infinitely safer than one not so protected. In the spring of the year the house fly begins to take on life. Eggs which were laid the preceding fall begin to hatch. At first the fly is only a little worm wriggling in some pile of filth. The eggs are usually laid and the grub developed in a manure pile or some mass of garbage or other filth. Before the grub develops into the fly it is easily destroyed. If everything in and about the house were kept scrupulously clean, and if every manure pile were kept carefully screened or covered so as to protect it from flies, there would be no difficulty in preventing the fly nuisance. The most effective way to accomplish this is to destroy the breeding places. The importance of this may be seen when it is considered that one fly produces one hundred and twenty-five millions or more of its kind in one season.

Stables.—Manure is by far the commonest material in which the fly lays her eggs. All stables should be kept scrupulously clean. No manure should be allowed to accumulate where it will be exposed to flies for even a few minutes. Immediately after it is dropped by an animal, it should be removed and covered.

Manure may be treated with considerable quantities of lime without interfering with its fertilizing value, and in this way the development of the eggs laid in it by the flies can be practically prevented. The floors of stables should be thoroughly [647] flushed with water at least once in every twenty-four hours.

Privy Vaults.—Human excrement also affords an excellent breeding place for flies. In army camps the latrines are the points from which much infection is transmitted to troops, and thousands of the men have lost their lives by contracting typhoid fever transmitted in this manner. During the summer time all open vaults and dry closets should be treated continuously with lime, crude creolin or crude carbolic acid, and they should be carefully cleaned out at frequent intervals.

Garbage.—As a medium for the development of flies, garbage may be considered next in importance to excreta. The eggs of the fly hatch in about twenty-four hours, and garbage which is retained in the kitchen for that length of time may contain flies in the grub stage. To prevent this development, all garbage should be covered and pails should be emptied as often as possible. In country districts garbage should be burned in the kitchen or buried in the garden at frequent intervals, twenty-four hours being the maximum time it should be retained.

Vacant Lots.—Vacant lots frequently contain appreciable quantities of organic matter in a state of decomposition, affording favorable breeding places for flies. These vacant areas should be maintained in a state of scrupulous cleanliness.

Foodstuffs.—In order to prevent contamination of foodstuffs, all foods that are eaten in the raw state and all foods that are exposed for sale after having been cooked should be carefully protected from contact with flies, by screens or covers.

A point where rapid development of flies takes place is along the city's water front. This is due to the fact that many of the sewers do not discharge below the level of the water. All open drains should be eliminated, whether they be sewers, private house drains or drains from cess-pools.

Precautions to be Observed.—Keep the house free from flies. Every fly should be considered a possible disease carrier and should be destroyed.

Keep the windows of the house, especially the kitchen [648] windows, carefully screened during the spring, summer and autumn.

Protect children from exposure to flies, particularly children who are ill, and do not allow nursing bottles to be exposed to flies.

Protect milk and other foodstuffs from contact with flies.

Keep the garbage outside of the house, carefully covered.

Abolish open drains near dwelling places.

Stable manure should be frequently sprinkled with lime and kept covered.

Earth closets and privy vaults should be treated with lime, crude creolin or crude carbolic acid at frequent intervals.

Earth closets and privy vaults should be cleaned frequently in order to prevent excrement accumulating to an undue extent.

To Kill Flies.—Dissolve one dram of bichromate of potash in two ounces of water, add a little sugar to this solution and put some of it in shallow dishes and place about the house. Sticky fly paper and fly traps may also be used.

To clean the room where there are many flies, burn pyrethrum powder (Persian insect powder). This stupefies the flies and in this condition they may be swept up and burned.

Probably the best and simplest fly killer is a weak solution of formaldehyde in water (two teaspoonfuls to the pint). This solution should be placed in plates or saucers throughout the house. Ten cents' worth of formaldehyde, obtained in the drug store, will last an ordinary family all summer. Don't smell formaldehyde in the pure state; it is very pungent and strong. In the solution of the strength used for flies it has no offensive smell. It is fatal to disease organisms, and is practically non-poisonous except to insects. Flies will not stay in the house when this solution is around.

Moths.—Late spring and early summer is the time to guard against moths and beetles. Many of these fabric-destroying insects are brought into the house on flowers. [649]

May and June are especially bad months, as both moths and beetles are only dangerous to fabrics in their young or grub stage.

These insects will destroy almost anything from coarse rugs to the finest of ball gowns and dress suits. Carpets that are rarely swept and garments that are seldom disturbed are most liable to damage.

The substitution of the frequently removed and easily cleaned rugs for carpets will greatly lessen the danger from the destructive moth and beetle grubs. Carpets laid on tight floors are much less liable to injury than where numerous cracks furnish safe retreats for the insects. Tarred paper under a carpet is an excellent preventive.

All clothes presses should be thoroughly cleaned at frequent intervals. The garments should be removed, aired and vigorously brushed. Any larvæ which are not dislodged in this way should be destroyed. It is a bad plan to keep odds and ends of woolen or other materials in attics where these pests can breed and thus spread to more valuable articles.

Spraying with benzine two or three times during hot weather is a good way of preventing injury to furniture or carriage upholstery and other articles which are in storage or not in use for a long time. If you are certain that woolens and furs are free from the pests they may be stored in safety by placing them in tight paste board boxes and sealing the covers firmly with gummed paper.

Both moths and carpet beetles are harmless at a temperature of 40 degrees Fahrenheit—a fact very well known to advantage by the large fur storage companies. They cannot survive furthermore a temperature of 120 decrees if subjected to it for about twenty minutes.

What Physicians are Doing.—It is desirable that the ordinary non-medical individual should know what the science of medicine is doing and what it is accomplishing.

During the past fifteen years the art of curing and preventing disease has taken on giant strides. The man or woman most ready to question the accomplishments and the ability of the humble family physician or the [650] motive of the science of medicine, is the one who appreciates least that it is due to the skill and intelligence of the medical men of to-day that he owes his comfort, his health, and his freedom from pestilence, plague and disease. Unthinking people laud and praise some upstart whose ability lies in his faculty to fool the gullible, or they will rush to seek the false aid of some nondescript science, because it is popular and well advertised, while they pass by or ignore the men whose labors have made the world what it is, and who alone possess the ability to intelligently wage the battle in the interest of humanity against disease.

The medical profession has repeatedly pointed out that there are, on an average, six hundred thousand lives lost every year in the United States from preventable disease and accidents. Six hundred thousand lives which medical science has at hand the remedy to save, but which the medical profession sacrificed because of inadequate legislation. Few people can comprehend just what six hundred thousand lives mean. Let us put it in another way. There are destroyed by preventable disease and accidents every day American lives equal in number to the crews of two battle ships, equal in three months to more than the total combined numbers of the Army and Navy of the United States; equal in one year to more than the total number of lives lost in all our wars since the Declaration of Independence.

The *Titanic* disaster shocked the public for a moment, and seemed to impress them as though it was a terrible and unheard of waste of good human lives. Yet in the loss of life due to preventable causes we have in this country every day in the year a destruction of our citizens exceeding in magnitude that which occurred when the *Titanic* sank. Think of it! A *Titanic* disaster a day, and yet the public does not rise up and demand in a spirit of anger and determination that steps be taken at once to put an end to this appalling and unnecessary waste of lives.

Under modern hygienic conditions, the average length of existence for an individual in Great Britain has increased ten years in the last half century. Among all the enlightened and advanced nations, the expectation of the individual for long survival is greater. Since the appearance of [651] uncheckable and epidemic disorders is less frequent and the percentage of cures is greater.

Since quarantine has been regularly established and the sewage system made efficient in large cities, and since the sanitary plumbing laws have been made compulsory, the general death rate has decreased enormously. These regulations have been the product of regularly educated medical or sanitary experts. No 'ism or 'ology has ever established any scientific principle which has contributed to the general welfare of the people. We no longer fear the plague, or typhus or yellow fever, cholera, diphtheria, typhoid, consumption, and other diseases which once were a constant menace to the race. The plague, for example, is practically limited to the Far East, where modern methods cannot evidently be introduced efficiently. At one time it periodically devastated Europe, where it cannot now get a foothold because of the introduction of sanitary systems and hygienic principles.

Tetanus or lockjaw and hydrophobia are now amenable to cure while formerly all cases were practically fatal. The mortality of diphtheria has been reduced more than fifty per cent. Antiseptic precautions in surgical cases, first introduced by the famous surgeon, Lord Lister, have made possible and successful operations that formerly could not be undertaken, thus broadening the whole field of surgical possibilities. The Boer war and the war with Spain proved this truth in a way that could not be denied. Smallpox is almost a medical curiosity in New York City, where it once was a scourge. The mortality of childbirth has been reduced to about one-fifth of what it was by the introduction of antiseptics and anesthetics. The new methods of making and preparing drugs, the sterilization and inspection of milk, the methods devised for the care of and preparation of infant foods have all enormously contributed to checking disease, to preventing disease, and to increasing the length of life and its happiness.

These are all facts which may be proved by any one, no matter how incompetent they may be. If we were to give up all these hard earned victories, cease to investigate or experiment, deny the existence of disease, and depend [652] upon the questionable methods of hysterical emotionalists we would soon find ourselves facing all the horrors of the past. Can we afford to lose the priceless benefits we have achieved and are attaining? Can we sit still and permit the profession of medicine, which has always contained the best of the race in its membership, the best intellects, the most sympathetic and unselfish characters, the noblest and most steadfast souls, to be maligned and assailed, to have its means of well-doing assaulted and threatened, when we know that it should be supported and protected for the sake of all it has done in the past in the interest of humanity?

Every mother should be acquainted with these facts so that she may lend her influence in behalf of honest effort and honest inquiry.

The following summary comprises a brief review of what medicine has been doing in the recent past:

Radium.—This element was discovered about fifteen years ago by Professor and Mme. Curie. It possesses the wonderful property of giving out inexhaustible stores of energy. It virtually possesses the property of perpetual motion. Professor Becquerel was the first one to suggest that it might possess therapeutic or healing powers. The suggestion came to him in a curious way. He carried a tube of radium in his vest pocket and was severely burnt as a consequence. The incident suggested to him that, if radium could attack healthy tissue in such a short time, it should be able to similarly attack diseased tissue. Experiments were soon instituted, and are still being conducted to exactly define its curative value and scope.

It was hailed as a cure for cancer and other serious conditions, but we have found that it is not a cure for these ailments. It is, however, exceedingly valuable in the treatment of certain skin diseases. In lupus, epithelial tumors, ulcers, papillomata, angiomata and pruritus, it is being widely and successfully used. It was later discovered that it can quickly kill disease-producing bacteria. It is also well known that it will efficiently purify water.

X-Ray Treatment and X-Ray Diagnosis.—Professor Roentgen gave to the world an exceedingly valuable discovery [653] in the X-Ray. He discovered that a certain form of electrical energy, when applied in a certain way, would produce shadows that differentiated between a certain degrees of opacity. For example, it would, if directed upon the human hand, produce shadows that clearly indicated whether the substance through which the rays passed was bone or muscle. The chief value of the X-Rays has been found to be this property rather than any healing value which has been attributed to them. The fact that these shadows can be photographed has rendered them of supreme value in surgery and medicine. Previously it was essential that the surgeon should depend upon his own diagnosis, upon what he could learn from his sense of touch and from surrounding conditions. With the X-Rays at his disposal he can quite eliminate the personal equation. His pictures are precise and mathematically accurate; he can prove the truth of his diagnosis before he cuts. We can take pictures of fractured bones and from what we learn we can immediately tell how they should be set to attain the very best results. We can actually tell if there is a stone in the kidney before we subject the patient to a serious operation. We can actually take pictures of the stomach at various stages of digestion and tell what disease affects the individual with a degree of precision that was not possible before the X-Rays were introduced. These examples only suggest its use. There are a multiplicity of uses for these as yet unknown rays which have greatly aided in diagnosis and consequently in successful treatment.

Aseptic Surgery.—The utility of the aseptic principle in surgery was demonstrated by the Japanese army surgeons during the war with Russia in 1904-1905. Their success in preventing deaths from suppurating wounds amazed the world. Their method was to discard the use of antiseptics and to depend upon absolutely clean instruments, dressings and hands. The most terrible wounds healed under this method without festering. This is, of course, the method in vogue to-day all over the civilized world. The Japanese did not discover aseptic surgery, but they were the first to put it to actual test in a large [654] way. The old method was to depend upon drugs to kill the germs which might find their way into wounds and operations. To-day we prevent the germs from getting into the wound and depend upon nature to do the rest.

New Anesthetics.—Several important advances have been made in methods of giving anesthetics and in the nature of the products used. Temporary unconsciousness with electricity was induced in 1909 by Dr. Stephane Leduc. Stovaine was invented by Dr. Jonnesco, of Bucharest. He injected it into the spinal cord after the method made famous by Biers with cocaine in 1899. Dr. W. S. Schley invented novocaine for the same purpose. Temporary unconsciousness was accomplished by the use of epsom salts injected into the spinal cord by Dr. Samuel J. Meltzer. All of these efforts to discover a harmless anesthetic by spinal injection were made possible by investigations and experiments of Dr. J. Leonard Corning, of New York, who worked along this line as far back as 1885. The most revolutionary discovery, however, was that of Dr. S. J. Meltzer at the Rockefeller Institute, New York, when he inserted a tube into the windpipe, through which he pumped the anesthetic into the lungs. While doing this he at the same time pumped oxygen to aerate the blood, thus ensuring the patient against possible accident during the course of difficult and tedious operations on the lungs and heart.

Vaccine in Typhoid Fever.—Inasmuch as typhoid fever has played an important part in the conduct of all wars, it has always been a source of much careful study by military and naval surgeons in every civilized country in the world. We had not, however, reached a stage when it was possible to hope for its extermination until medical science began to appreciate the possibilities of vaccine therapy. The Cuban, Boer and Russian wars, because of the terrible experiences of the soldiers with typhoid in each of them, stimulated inquiry along the line of discovering a serum of vaccine that would be effectual against it. American, British, French and Japanese military and naval surgeons instituted experiments simultaneously to discover an anti-typhoid vaccine. In the fall of 1909, American army surgeons were experimenting [655] with a serum at Washington and on Governor's Island with success, but the first public announcement of an absolutely successful vaccine was made by Captain Vincent of the French navy on June 20th, 1910, before the Académie de Medicine in Paris. The final success of the anti-typhoid serum has been conclusively proved by elaborate tests upon soldiers and sailors in many nations.

It is difficult for the ordinary individual to appreciate the significance and importance of a discovery of this character and magnitude. When one thinks calmly of the thousands and thousands of men who have lost their lives during wars because of typhoid epidemics, and of the thousands of others who have returned home practically invalided for life from the same cause, it is possible to, at least, conceive of the benefit to the race such a discovery promises. And when we learn that the discovery is a product of the same principle or method which gave to the world a cure for smallpox, diphtheria and syphilis, we must begin to believe that the medical profession is on the path which is unlimited in its field of promise so far as efficient treatment is concerned. Yet to-day we have people who do not believe in vaccination or in anti-diphtheritic serum. We may not live to see the time, but it is not far distant in the opinion of men qualified to speak with authority, when every disease will be amenable to the serum therapy, and when drugs will virtually be discarded by the human race.

"606."—One of the most important discoveries in the history of medicine was recently given to the world by Dr. Paul Ehrlich.

He called it "606," because it was the 606th experiment he had made with the same end in view. It was designed with the purpose of curing the most terrible disease known to man, syphilis. The name of the remedy is salvarsan. That it will do all that was first claimed for it is still doubtful, but salvarsan and its improvements, neosalvarsan, etc., are accepted by the profession as by far the best treatment yet devised for this dread disease. It points the way for improvement along the same line to an ultimate specific.

[656]

Transplanting the Organs of Dead Men Into Living Men.—To take from a recently dead individual a kidney, or a bone, or an artery, and by immersing them in certain fluids thereby keeping them alive indefinitely, and later transplanting them in the body of a living individual so that they will continue to live and perform their function in the new environment, is a revolutionary and a seemingly incredible performance. Yet Dr. Alexis Carrel of the Rockefeller Institute, New York, has accomplished this wonderful task. The smallest imagination can picture the possibilities of this kind of surgery, but, inasmuch as the discovery is so recent and the opportunities for testing it upon human beings are so relatively few, that time alone can tell how far it may be possible to go.

Anti-Meningitis Serum.—Another important discovery that has emanated from the Rockefeller Institute is the Anti-Meningitis serum. The death rate from spinal meningitis, before the introduction of the serum, was 70 per cent., the use of the serum has reduced this percentage to 30. We owe this important contribution to Dr. Simon Flexner.

A Serum for Malaria Now Possible.—Dr. C. C. Bass, of Tulane University, has succeeded in extracting malaria-producing parasites from human blood and keeping them alive in test tubes. This feat had been long attempted but never before with success. The significance of this achievement is that it is the first step toward preparing a serum that will give immunity to malaria.

www.ingramcontent.com/pod-product-compliance
Lightning Source LLC
LaVergne TN
LVHW051125080426
835510LV00018B/2239